Is the U.S.A. in Prophecy?

S. FRANKLIN LOGSDON

ZONDERVAN PUBLISHING HOUSE
GRAND RAPIDS, MICHIGAN

Is the U. S. A. in Prophecy?
Copyright © 1968 by Zondervan Publishing House
Grand Rapids, Michigan

First printing.................1968
Second printing........March, 1969
Third printing......September, 1969
Fourth printing..............1970

Printed in the United States of America

PREFACE

THE MATTER TREATED in this volume has been incubating in the author's mind for many years, and the increasingly frequent question, "Is the U.S.A. in prophecy?" has been the chief prompting to reduce our ponderings to print.

It seems strange that more consideration has not been accorded this subject. As I have spoken on the theme in cities across the country, there has been much interest evidenced, with the attendance swelled not infrequently to an overflow. People want to know, as never before, just what God has to say about our great nation. And — what does He have to say?

The prevailing attitude in this connection seems to be, not that God has not spoken, but where and how has He spoken? How may one know?

This is not an enigma. If God has spoken on any matter, He wants His people to know about it. Revelation is for information. Such information, with the assistance of the Holy Spirit's guidance, is obtained by studying. Studying is searching. This we are commanded to do.

Lethargic minds, of course, would prefer matters simplified for them. Few in our day, in the rank and file of professing Christians, know the ecstatic joy, the rapturous pleasure, of fitting together the scattered pieces of biblical references to form the revealed whole. However, when the proper "pieces" are in their proper places, the picture emerges clearly and convincingly.

We launch into the subject of this book with the comfortable assumption that the omniscient God, looking down the corridors of time, and concerning Himself so prominently with the Gentile nations, did not overlook the one nation He has blessed above all others.

We proceed logically and reasonably to extract from divine Revelation the descriptions of an unnamed nation. Then, deductively, giving careful attention to relationships, endeavors, accomplishments and character, we press toward a crystallization for identification.

Applying basic truths relative to God's dealings with nations, we observe the tendencies and trends of national behavior on the part of one nation biblically described. We note how, though singularly blessed, this prophesied nation incurs the displeasure and eventual indignation of the Most High God, and how she places herself in line for His severe judgment.

We notice also how she diminishes in world influence and deteriorates internally. Boasting of superb power and mighty defenses, but living lustfully and godlessly, she finally is plunged into desolation.

Because the details of this whole scriptural portrayal of an endtime nation bears such a striking and convincing resemblance to the U. S. A., one more courageous than the author would forthrightly declare, "She's the one." However, we prefer restraint of dogmatism, in spite of deep and definite personal convictions, and simply commend this thought-provoking treatise to the meditative reader's prayerful consideration.

We believe it will prove to be a timely and useful presentation, and we earnestly entreat the Lord of the harvest to arouse His dilatory workers through it. While they sleep, the enemy sows his tares of unrest, violence and revolution.

Lenin, in pleading for loyalty to the communist cause, said, "A successful revolution cannot be had through a part-time endeavor."

How infinitely more does Christianity, with its matchless provision for a noble life, a victorious death and a blissful hereafter, deserve wholeheartedness and unswerving devotion, thus guaranteeing the continued favor of God! For righteousness alone exalts a nation. But, alas, such devotion is but faintly evident today and appears to be fading ominously. Spiritual decadence has clouded we observe the tendencies and trends of national behavior on the the horizon with alarming portents while complacency prevails.

Said Dr. Paul Rees, "America must be stabbed awake. The blackness of the blackest night is settling about us. The blackest part of the picture is the inaction of Christian America."

Israel sowed to the wind and reaped the whirlwind (Hosea 8:7). How awesome and terrifying may be the final result of America's careless course. This should become apparent in the following pages.

CONTENTS

Preface

1. Is the U.S.A. in Prophecy?...................... 7
2. Identifying Unspecified Entities..................... 10
3. A Probable Lead 11
4. A Search for the Key........................... 13
5. The Divine Appeal............................. 16
6. Is the "Woman" a City?....................... 17
7. Divine Indignation 19
8. Blending Colors............................... 21
9. Babylon's Mother 23
10. Cup of Gold.................................. 24
11. Cosmopolitan Country 26
12. The Youngest Nation........................... 28
13. A Nation of Wealth............................ 29
14. Prestigiously Great 30
15. Amazing Attainments........................... 32
16. Voice of Influence 33
17. Excellent Fortifications......................... 34
18. World Involvements 37
19. Foreign Aid................................... 38
20. Blatant Covetousness 40
21. Epicurean Traits............................... 41
22. Spiritual Decadence............................ 43
23. Egotistically Blind............................. 44
24. Dispossessed 46
25. Lack of Embellishments......................... 48
26. Instrument of Judgment......................... 50
27. Enemy Characterized 52
28. Nature of Attack 53
29. Time of Development........................... 55
30. A Prominent Name 57
31. A Recapitulation............................... 58
32. Not an Empty Theory 60
33. A Glimpse of Modern America................... 62

1. IS THE U.S.A. IN PROPHECY?

"WE WILL BURY YOU!"

Thus roared Nikita Khrushchev in the epithet of the ages, as he poured forth one of his innumerable invectives against the U. S. A. To most Americans it was but the outburst of an irresponsible individual, scarcely worthy of notice, and was met with lightness and even laughter.

But let us not forget that Mr. Khrushchev was speaking as the leader of the increasingly powerful Soviet Union. Representing as he was the avowed enemy of the United States, there is no doubt that he was reflecting the feeling, if not the united intent, of his compatriots. Nor is there any reason to believe, with the passing of Khrushchev from the scene, that the Soviets have abandoned, or even lessened, their insidious animosity and hostility against our country. Quite the opposite.

The threatening statement issued by Mr. Khrushchev has all but faded from the minds of our citizenry—dismissed as exorbitant language or even as a tyranny of words. Our only point in reviving it in this treatise is that it possibly may prove, when the facts are assembled, to coincide with the authoritative prophecy of God Himself.

Our presentation of this subject, however, is no attempt to be spectacular. It is simply a bold endeavor to face up to some staggering and alarming suggestions. Nor is the question raised in this first chapter rhetorical, for the answer is not immediately evident. Therefore, our consideration is not so much an exposition as an investigation—an exploration of solemn and serious portents.

In dealing with prophetical matters, we are well advised to avoid the rash and groundless, the speculative and conjectural. But it is of equal importance that we do not allow prejudice and tradition, misinformation and bigotry to contract the cornea of our eyes when light does shine out of darkness.

Now to the point. If you ask, Is the U. S. A. mentioned by name in prophecy? the answer, of course, is "No." But, if you ask, Is the U. S. A. in the framework of prophecy? the answer is an unqualified "Yes," as the following Bible references will reveal.

These references are clearly and distinctly universal in scope, and therefore embrace the U. S. A. This fact established, in due course we may move from the general to the specific in an attempt to focus the spotlight of prophecy upon a single nation.

1. In a panoramic declaration of prophetic intention, God says, "This is the purpose which is purposed on the whole earth" (Isaiah 14:26). The U. S. A. obviously is part of the "whole earth," and would have to be in the framework of prophecy.

2. In the same projection of plans, God adds, "and this is the hand that is stretched out upon all the nations." Of course, the U. S. A. is one of the "all nations," and God's hand will be stretched out upon her.

3. "Though I make a full end of all nations whither I have scattered thee, yet will I not make a full end of thee [Israel]" (Jeremiah 30:11).

Israel is the only nation with which the infinite God has had a vital relationship (Amos 3:2). Israel will be restored to divine blessing and usefulness. All other nations are scheduled to disappear. Meanwhile, the descendants of Jacob are scattered among many nations. These nations, the text makes clear, will come to a "full end."

The U. S. A contains a great number of these dispersed Jews. Since God has declared that all such nations will come to an end, therefore, the U. S. A. will have her national existence terminated by the hand of God—sometime.

4. "I will execute vengeance in anger and fury upon the nations (none excepted), such as they have not heard" (Micah 5:15). This is the hand of divine judgment which will strike when apostasy shall have reached the universal saturation point. Fast becoming spiritually decadent, the U. S. A. is apparently included in the above prophecy.

5. "And all the nations shall see my judgment . . ." (Ezekiel 39:21). Here again, we note the all-inclusive adjective. Where is there the slightest glimmer of assurance that our country can possibly escape the fearful consequences of forgetting and forsaking God who has lavished upon us His abounding goodness and lovingkindness?

6. "For the day of the Lord is near upon all the nations . . . and they shall be as though they had not been" (Obadiah 15, 16). This is a declarative statement, authentic, authoritative and prophetic. There is no indication of an exception.

7. "And I will overthrow the throne of kingdoms, and I will destroy the strength of the kingdoms of the nations . . ." (Haggai 2:22). The context clearly proves that this prophecy is yet future—how far beyond contemporary times is not known. There seems to be no comfortable reason to think that it cannot be comparatively soon.

8. ". . . I have put my spirit upon him [Christ]: he shall bring judgment to the nations" (Isaiah 42:1). He does not say that a single nation shall be exempt, so this prophecy must include the U. S. A.

9. "The lion is come up from his thicket, and the destroyer of the nations is on his way . . ." (Jeremiah 4:7). The lion coming up from his thicket, and the "adversary the devil as a roaring lion" (I Peter 5:8) are expressions of prevailing lawlessness and rampant godlessness. This, according to the prophecy, signals the soon coming of the Lord to put down all rebellion. He will then "destroy" the nations. Once again, there is no exception. Thus, the U. S. A. would have to be included.

10. "Why do the nations rage, and the people imagine a vain thing? . . . He that sitteth in the heavens shall laugh; the Lord shall have them in derision" (Psalm 2:1, 4). The word "rage" means "to be tumultuous," and springs from a root suggesting commotion, restlessness, disquietness, noise and trouble. When the omniscient God asks why these conditions shall obtain among the nations, it is not that He does not know. The thought is, What do the nations expect to gain through tumultuous demonstrations and widespread commotion, through restlessness and noise? These conditions are becoming commonplace in America. It would be most unwise to declare that the U. S. A. is not in prophecy, that the Lord did not see these conditions existing here as well as in the other nations of the world.

Actually, it is unthinkable that the God who knows the end from the beginning would pinpoint such small nations as Libya, Egypt, Ethiopia and Syria in the prophetic declaration and completely overlook the wealthiest and most powerful nation on the earth. Too long have we evaded the question. Too long have we summarily grouped our country with the so-called revived Roman Empire. Too long have we persisted in terming the U. S. A. in prophecy as one of the "lion's cubs," thus giving her but an inferential mention in the shadow of a diminishing Britain.

2. *IDENTIFYING UNSPECIFIED ENTITIES*

PROPHETIC ENTITIES, not specifically designated in prophecy, may be identified by representations or by descriptions.

Representations. The Lord Jesus Christ, the King of righteousness, is represented by Melchisedec (Hebrews 7:1). Israel, the ten northern tribes, is represented by Ephraim (Hosea 11:3). Dispersed Israel is represented by Lo-ammi, the second son of Hosea and Gomer (Hosea 1:9). Elijah is represented by John the Baptizer (Luke 1:17). The Devil is represented as the old dragon (Revelation 12:9). These are but a few illustrations, but sufficient to establish our point.

Descriptions. These are even more numerous than representations. Metaphors and similes abound in the Scriptures. They sparkle with appropriate grandeur when setting forth the Son of God made flesh, who came to save us from our sins. He is described as the seed of the woman, the virgin-born, the ancient of days, the Lamb of God, the door, the bread of life, the light of the world, the righteous servant, the branch, the bright and morning star, the water of life, the second man, the last Adam, to mention but a few.

Satan, too, is set forth in the Scriptures by myriads of descriptions. He is referred to as the serpent, the lying spirit, the son of the morning, the deceiver, the tempter, the enemy, the unclean spirit, the foul spirit, the angel of light, the god of this world, the prince of the power of the air, the angel of the bottomless pit, the great red dragon, the old serpent, the accuser, the murderer, the liar and the father of lies.

The Church is spoken of as a building (Ephesians 2:21), a bride (Ephesians 5:30), and a body (Colossians 1:18).

The coming world dictator is set forth as the little horn, the king, the man of sin, the son of perdition, the wicked one, the Antichrist, and the beast.

Jerusalem is described as the city of David, the holy city, the city of peace, the city of truth and the city of the King. Any one of these would be sufficient identification for those conversant with the language of Scripture.

It is interesting also to note how proper names are used as descriptive designations. Baalim is employed for idolatry (Jeremiah 2:23), David for the Lord Jesus Christ (Hosea 3:5), "the swelling of the Jordan" for emergencies (even death itself—Jeremiah 12:5), and "Jerusalem that is above," meaning heaven (Galatians 4:26).

In this connection observe that the two witnesses of the Tribulation "shall lie in the street of the great city, which spiritually is called Sodom and Egypt, where also our Lord was crucified" (Revelation 11:8). If Jerusalem is given such an unbelievable descriptive appellation as Sodom, it should not surprise us to discover a strange proper noun to describe the U. S. A. in prophecy.

We must, therefore, search for a designation or a description which in a convincing manner fits her. By description, we can identify people, places and things. Thus, it should not be impossible, or even too difficult, to identify a nation in this manner.

3. A PROBABLE LEAD

WE NEED TO HAVE ETCHED upon our minds a very prominent teaching in the Bible which may lend assistance in the pursuance of our subject. It is the *Babylon Doctrine*. It involves infinitely more than the casual Bible reader would imagine. Emerging in the tenth chapter of Genesis, it extends to the nineteenth chapter of Revelation. It actually commences with a man by the name of Nimrod, about whom it is said, "He began to be a mighty one in the earth" (Genesis 10:8).

Thus, beginning in the days of Nimrod in the early chapters of the Bible and continuing through the Scriptures to the heavenly "alleluias" of final defeat in Revelation 19, the Babylon doctrine has an impressive place. The word "Babylon" is synonymous with confusion, and Satan is its author (I Corinthians 14:33). It is, in one form or another, a diabolical attempt to contradict all that God says and to counteract all that He does.

This Babylon matter is comprehended within three designations: (1) *Historical Babylon* in Genesis 11; (2) *Ecclesiastical Babylon* in Revelation 17; and (3) *Political Babylon* in Revelation 18. Historical Babylon will ultimately manifest itself in two imposing branches, viz., the false church and a powerful God-forsaking nation. These will suffer defeat at the hands of Him who will not tolerate ungodly usurpation of His royal rights and divine prerogatives.

Historical "B" is symbolized by a monumental tower, *Ecclesiastical "B"* by a mystical woman, and *Political "B"* by a mighty city. The aim is, respectively, to reach heaven, to rob heaven, and to reject heaven. The proposal of the first was a common language. The proposal of the second is a common worship. The proposal of the third is a common privilege — one speech, one church, one society. The Utopian dream, in each instance, may be experessed as (1) a cohesion of people, (2) a commingling of churches, and (3) a confluence of power—to stay together, to worship together, to excel all others.

In the case of Historical Babylon, God felled the tower, confounded the tongues and scattered the people.

In the case of Ecclesiastical or Religious Babylon, the Beast (Antichrist) will hate the "harlot," outlaw religion, and finally kill the "woman"; that is, he will destroy the final development of organized religion.

In the case of prophetical, Political Babylon, trials will plague the earth, the economy will crash; the great city will be made desolate.

THE CONFUSION AND CONFOUNDING OF BABYLON

"Babylon the Great is fallen, is fallen" (Rev. 14:8).

DESIGNATION	SYMBOL	PROPOSAL	UTOPIAN DREAM
Historical "B" (Gen. 11)	A Monumental Tower To Reach Heaven	A Common Language One Speech	Cohesion of People To Stay Together
Ecclesiastical "B" (Rev. 17)	A Mystical Woman To Rob Heaven	A Common Worship One Church	Commingling of Churches To Get Together
Political "B" (Rev. 18)	A Mighty City To Reject Heaven	A Common Privilege One Society	Confluence of Power To Excel All Others
Defeated "B" (I Cor. 15:25)	God Fells the Tower Beast Hates Harlot Trials Plague Earth	Tongues Confounded Religion Outlawed Economy Crashes	People Are Scattered Woman Is Killed City Made Desolate
HISTORICAL BABYLON eventuates in		Religious Babylon—The False Church (Rev. 17) Political Babylon—The Great Nation (Rev. 18)	

The alert reader will have sensed the many suggested involvements in this highly condensed outline. Building a tower to reach heaven suggests the blatant doctrine of "salvation by works"—the age-long claim that, "If I do the best I can, or if I keep the Ten Commandments, or if I observe the golden rule, I'm sure I'll reach heaven at last." This is a clear contradiction of the authoritative Word of God. "By grace ye are saved through faith, and that not of yourselves; it is the gift of God, not of works lest any man should boast" (Ephesians 2:8).

Babylonism is not only a system of contradictory works, but a scheme of unmitigated robbery, depriving the infinite God of the praise and glory due His holy name, denying His power and His operations. Babylonism is also a satanic willfulness which rejects divine intervention and seeks to solve its own problems and to build its own arrangement of things, giving no thought to God's will or way. "The world *we* are building" is a current expression, illustrative of this present climate or attitude.

The proposal is that of a one-church, one-world development, which, through ecumenicity, unionization, common markets and the United Nations, is currently gaining rapid momentum. It will all culminate in the religionist's fondest dream and in the Devil's amazing success—the ultimate in monumentalizing unbelief among men. But "he that sitteth in the heavens shall laugh; the Lord shall have them in derision" (Psalm 2:4).

God, who stables His battalions in the skies, from before the foundation of the world has set the exact time for each of His inevitable victories over these forces of unrighteousness. He will eliminate utterly the false church through the agency of Antichrist (Revelation 17:17). He will also completely destroy a powerful endtime nation which is spiritually called Babylon (Revelation 18:10).

This will be an eternal memorial to Christ's complete triumph over Babylon's deception and tyranny, both in the religious and political realms. This will occasion the second greatest of all celebrations (the greatest being the exhibition of the redeemed Church as recorded in Ephesians 2:7) as a thunderous chorus jubilantly cries, "Hallelujah; for the Lord God omnipotent reigneth" (Revelation 19:6).

4. A SEARCH FOR THE KEY

Now, WE WILL EXPLORE the possibility of finding a key in this Babylon doctrine as we search for the answer to the question, Is the U.S.A. in prophecy? Admittedly, there are some problems to be encountered, but they are not too difficult to solve. The *first* one we meet is the plurality of applications for the word "Babylon." The following may offer some clarification:

Historical Babylon — A system
Political Babylon — An Empire
Municipal Babylon — A city
Prophetical Babylon— { a. The World Church
                      { b. An endtime nation

It would be even more difficult meeting these plural designations were it not for the fact that such situations are found in many other areas of scriptural consideration. As an illustration in point, the word "world" has various connotations in Scripture. The context, however, always indicates whether the meaning is (1) the sphere on which we live, or (2) the human family (which God so loved that He gave His only Son, that whosoever believeth in Him should never perish), or (3) the satanic system which is designed to keep people content without God, and which the believer is not to love" (I John 2:15).

The context likewise will enable us to ascertain the proper application of the word "Babylon." We will know whether the Holy Spirit is referring to historical, political, municipal or prophetical Babylon. If this were not true, we would face hopeless confusion in trying to discern prophetical declarations.

The *second* obstacle which presents itself is this: Is prophetical Babylon a nation or a city? In Jeremiah 50 and 51, it is presented as a nation; in Revelation 18, it is a city. But there is no contradiction, indeed cannot be! Nations are referred to by the chief or capital city. Thus, we speak of Washington for the U. S. A., Moscow for the Soviet Union, Paris for France, London for England, Saigon for South Vietnam, etc.

The Journal Herald of Dayton, Ohio, May 14, 1968, captioned its report of the Vietnam peace talks in Paris in this manner: WASHINGTON AND HANOI ARE SEATED AT THE TABLE. When Jesus cried out, "O Jerusalem, Jerusalem!" He clearly meant the nation. A few Bible quotations will suffice to prove that prophetical Babylon is a nation:

"How is Babylon a desolation among the nations" (Jeremiah 50:23).

"Shall empty her land" (Jeremiah 51:2).

"Her cities are a desolation" (Jeremiah 51:43).

"I will punish the king of Babylon and his land" (Jeremiah 50:18).

The parent verse for the Revelation 18 reference to Babylon as a city is found in Jeremiah 51:6, in which context it is irrefutably a nation. Thus, prophetical Babylon is a nation and not a city.

The *third* problem to be faced in attempting to find a key in the Babylon doctrine is that of determining whether or not the Babylon prophecy in Jeremiah 50 and 51 actually projects into the remote future—to what is commonly called "the endtime."

Much prophecy has a near and a distant application. All must agree to this. But some claim that all references to Babylon in these Jeremiah chapters are historical in character; hence, already fulfilled. Others maintain that there is convincing, even irrefutable, evidence of remote prophecy in these Jeremiah chapters—much that to this date definitely has not been fulfilled. Proof of this latter claim is most relevant to our consideration. Ponder the following:

> In those days and at that time, saith the Lord, the children of Israel shall come, they and the children of Judah together, going and weeping; they will go and seek the Lord their God (Jeremiah 50:4).

> In those days, and in that time, saith the Lord, the iniquity [rebellion] of Israel shall be sought for, and there shall be none (Jeremiah 50:20).

These prophecies, beyond any possibility of contradiction, are of future fulfillment when the promised regathering and restoration will find Israel and Judah (once and for so long a time divided) re-united and reconciled to Jehovah-God in the land which was promised them through Abraham. There is an impressive number of such evidences of remote prophecy in these Jeremiah chapters.

This fact of unfulfilled prophecies in Jeremiah 50 and 51 finds some very strong support in the divinely-employed expression, "Daughter of Babylon" (Jeremiah 51:33). Daughter of which Babylon? The Babylon Empire had no offspring as will the Roman Empire. The city had no prophesied successor. It is and must of necessity be understood to be the daughter or outgrowth of historical Babylon—that system of the ages with its God-rejecting tendencies and sacrilegious influences which, in the endtime, will eventuate in two imposing branches namely, *religious* Babylon, the ultimate of organized religious systems, and *political* or *eco-*

nomic Babylon, a nation of impressive and superior characteristics.

A corollary to bolster this "daughter" suggestion may be found in Jeremiah 4:31 where God speaks of the "daughter of Zion." Notice the similarity of expression. God was referring to the descendants of those whom He was then addressing. He was pointing out their sorrow and their woes, and the application carries through to contemporary times and even to a time yet in the future. The quotation reads as follows:

> . . . I have heard a voice as of a woman in travail, and the anguish as of her that bringeth forth her first child, the voice of the daughter of Zion, that bewaileth herself, that spreadeth her hands, saying, Woe is me now! for my soul is wearied because of murderers (Jeremiah 4:31).

Because God knew the end from the beginning, and the people did not, He pointed out to them the painful consequences their rebellion against Him would visit upon their descendants. Away back there in antiquity, God dipped into the future and revealed that He heard their posterity moaning and groaning under anti-semitic persecution. He heard every moan of the 500,000 who so recently starved to death in Poland. He heard every pitiful cry of the 6,000,000 who perished under the heel of Hitler.

When the facts of prophecy are properly and understandingly viewed in Jeremiah 50 and 51, what God says about the "Daughter of Babylon" is just as clear as that which He reveals about the "Daughter of Zion." And observe, the word "daughter" is in the singular. There are two extensions of Babylon—the religious and the political. The context makes it clear that the reference here to "daughter" connotes the political offspring, or the endtime nation being described.

5. THE DIVINE APPEAL

THE VERY BASIC IDEA in prophecy is that of our omniscient God setting forth in human expression what will transpire in the future. And it is remarkably noteworthy how He so specifically calls attention to one matter of stupendous consequence.

Quoting from Jeremiah 50:45, we read, "Therefore hear ye the counsel of the Lord that he hath taken against Babylon." He of course does not here suggest that we argue the matter, that we advance our opinions, that we evolve a spectacular thesis. No, He merely requests us to hear His counsel that He has taken against a certain Babylon, which, to all intents and purposes, appears to be an endtime nation, spiritually called Babylon. This counsel is prolifically stated in Jeremiah 50 and 51 and in Revelation 18.

In hearing this counsel of the Lord, one's undivided and prayerful attention is required. We would do well to emulate the attitude of Samuel, the Barnabas of the Old Testament, in saying, "Speak; for thy servant heareth" (I Samuel 3:10). And, in hearing, it is exceedingly important to understand that the near and remote aspects of the Babylon doctrine are interspersed throughout Jeremiah 50 and 51, with both historical Babylon and prophetical Babylon in view. A cursory glance will not produce the distinction. A novice may not detect the difference.

This, of course, would be just as true in differentiating between the "day of Jacob's trouble" in the past and the "day of Jacob's trouble" that is yet to come as we find them in Jeremiah. Both are there. Some do not see the difference. The same would be true in distinguishing between the immediate plagues and the remote plagues of the Great Tribulation as found in the book of Joel. Both are there. Some fail to note this as well. On the other hand, many who do clearly see these two distinctions, have given little or no attention to distinguishing between historical Babylon and prophetical Babylon in Jeremiah 50 and 51. Both likewise are there.

The burden of this presentation is to isolate and to correlate the prophetic elements of the remote kind in these Jeremiah contexts. Then, with the proper entity fixed in our minds, to learn what God says about the ultimate development and consequences.

6. IS THE "WOMAN" A CITY?

AT FIRST SIGHT, it would seem that the *woman* is indeed the *city,* for Revelation 17:18 reads after this manner, "The woman which thou sawest is that great city." But there should be no difficulty in understanding this passage if we properly regard the tense of the verb, the position of the verse in the context, and the usual terminology of Scripture.

Can seven swine be seven years? Can seven ears of corn be seven years in the calendar? Can the bread which Jesus held in His hand at the Last Supper actually be His body? Can seven heads be seven mountains? Can ten horns be ten kings? Then may the woman be the city. Let it be stated with the utmost simplicity that, whatever the answer is to the above questions, the same will be accurately true of this: Can the woman be the city? Because this simple question has not been properly answered, many maintain that there is one Babylon in Revelation 17 and 18. This might be construed as an evasive attitude. It certainly is not a satisfactory resolution of an important prophetic matter.

There seems to be no expression in the Hebrew or the Greek languages comparable with the English words, "symbolize," "typify" or "denote." When Joseph interpreted Pharaoh's dream of seven lean and seven fat kine and seven lean and seven full ears of corn, he conveyed to him the fact that the lean kine and lean ears of corn pointed to seven years of scarcity or famine, while the fat kine and full ears of corn meant seven years of prosperity. We have no problem understanding this. No further question need be raised.

Paul tells us that Jesus "took the bread; and when he had given thanks, he brake it, and said, Take, eat: this is my body which is broken for you" (I Corinthians 11:24). Our Roman Catholic friends and relatives believe with a passionate fervor that the bread *is* His body. They do not believe the swine and ears were years but they believe the bread *is* the body of Christ. It is precisely the same grammatical expression. But, note well the text — *He* took the bread. Did Christ take His own body? It was He who broke it. He Himself was the agent in the operation. Did He break His own body?

When some get to Revelation 17, they become confused with the same grammatical construction and imagine all sorts of things and evoke varying conclusions. "The seven heads are seven mountains" (v. 9). Are they? No, they *symbolize* seven mountains, and the word "mountain" symbolizes an empire or a nation. It is a political situation, not a geographical position. They are not the seven hills on which Rome sits, but seven heads of state over which Rome has influence.

With this well in mind, let us look at the statement, "And the woman which thou sawest is that great city . . ." (Revelation 17:

18). That we have identically the same grammatical construction here as noted above is crystal clear.

First of all, the verb is in the past tense—"which thou sawest." While verbs at times may be a source of trouble in dealing with prophetical matters, there is no problem here. The "woman" expires in verse 16. She is finished, gone! Completely disposed of, the "woman" cannot possibly be anything henceforth. It is a complete destruction. Smoke will ascend from the plain of Shinar forever as a memorial to her destruction (Revelation 19:3). Here is the record:

> And the ten horns which thou sawest upon the beast, these shall hate the whore [the composite church or religious Babylon] and shall make her desolate [non-operative] and naked [by stripping her of all privilege], and shall eat her flesh [expropriate her vast resources], and burn her with fire [eliminate her utterly] (Revelation 17:16; parenthetical notes are the author's).

So the "woman" or religious Babylon is no more. The terminology, then, of Revelation 17:18, consistent with the other similar constructions mentioned earlier, would mean, "The Woman which thou sawest symbolizes the great city." That is to say, as went the "woman," so shall go the "city." Or, saith the Lord, "As I have put down religious Babylon so shall I destroy political Babylon."

7. DIVINE INDIGNATION

NEUTRALITY HAS NO PLACE with Deity. God is either "with" or "against." Can antitheses be more striking? God speaks of being with His own and of being against the wicked. Jesus said to His own, "Go . . . and, lo, I am with you . . ." (Matthew 28: 19, 20). Jehovah said, "I am against thee, O Gog, the chief prince of Meshech and Tubal" (Ezekiel 38:3).

It is solemn, indeed, when the God of love must express utter contempt, such as, "Behold, I am against thee, O thou most proud, saith the Lord . . . I will visit thee" (Jeremiah 50:31). "Visit thee" means with judgment. This indicates the end of divine patience and blessing, and prophetical Babylon incurs the indignation of Deity. No such nation, regardless of its vaunted strength, can protect itself if God's hand of judgment is turned against it. All nations sooner or later will be judged, for God has said, ". . . I will make an end of all nations" (Jeremiah 30:11), but one prominent, powerful, once God-blessed Gentile nation is especially singled out for devastating judgment prior to all others, and this nation is spiritually called Babylon.

Those who are assuredly safe in the salvation which Christ has provided through His full and effective sacrifice give little attention to the meaning of divine indignation, and, of course, the careless, blinded unbeliever seldom entertains the possibility of such, but the indignation of God is the dreadful effect of His anger. Concerning the Day of the Lord (or the Great Tribulation), and particularly the battle of Armageddon, we read these sobering words,

> Come near, ye nations, to hear; and hearken, ye people: let the earth hear, and all that is therein: the world, and all things that come forth of it. For the indignation of the Lord is upon all nations, and his fury upon all their armies: he hath utterly destroyed them, he hath delivered them to the slaughter (Isaiah 34:1, 2).

During this prophesied period of outpoured judgment, God says to the saved Jews of that time, "Come, my people, enter thou into thy chambers, and shut thy doors about thee: hide thyself as it were for a little moment, until the indignation be overpast" (Isaiah 26:20). Like a devastating tornado passes but leaves wanton destruction in its train, just so the indignation of the Lord will pass, but the horrendous results will be imponderable.

Regarding the destruction of prophetical Babylon, here is a striking entry in the revealed plans, "The Lord hath opened his armoury, and hath brought forth the weapons of his indignation . . ." (Jeremiah 50:25).

"Hath opened" has a terrifying connotation. It does not mean to draw upon a storehouse or stockpile of death-dealing agents, but to throw widely open, as the bursting dykes let go the immeasurable floods. And the term, "weapons of his indignation," speaks of God's severest expression of wrath. This is not the empty palaver of a boulevard prognosticator, it is the promise of Him whose word cannot be broken. It shall come to pass.

Prior to this outburst of dreadful judgment, there will be a marvelous manifestation of divine mercy which "falleth as the gentle rain from heaven." It is the call for a modern exodus of Jews. Here is the record:

> And I heard another voice from heaven, saying, Come out of her, my people, that ye be not partakers of her sins, and that ye receive not of her plagues (Revelation 18:4).

Is this a call for the Church? No. A challenge for present-day believers? No. Of course, the Lord calls upon His people in every day to separate from all deception and confusion, from all that is contrary to His holiness, but the Church, the members of the body of Christ (Colossians 1:18), are not in view here. Not only will they have been caught up by this time, but the false church, the "whore" of Revelation 17, will be gone from the scene also. The alarm is divinely sounded for His saved people of the Tribulation period. Some Jeremiah passages are most explicit in this connection.

> Flee out of the midst of Babylon, and deliver every man his soul: be not cut off in her iniquity; for this is the time of the Lord's vengeance; he will render unto her a recompense (Jeremiah 51:6).

This perhaps will be a much-emphasized text for the 144,000 preachers the Lord will ordain for that day (Revelation 7:4). "Get thee out of the nation, [spiritually] called Babylon, which the Lord is going to destroy!" may be, conceivably, the pleading of these faithful preachers. It will be, in all probability, one of God's methods and means of getting the descendants of Jacob back into the land of Palestine.

And should the endtime nation that God has in view be the U. S. A., then it would mean that He will evacuate the Jews (at least those saved after the Church is raptured, together with all others who have believed the Gospel), even as He took righteous Lot out of Sodom before He let fall His hand of judgment upon that city. But whatever nation it may prove to be, out of it God will call all those who are His by faith in His salvation.

Those who will pack up and leave and go to Palestine will have a striking testimony. We read, "The voice of them that flee and escape out of the land of Babylon, to declare in Zion the vengeance of the Lord our God . . ." (Jeremiah 50:28).

8. BLENDING COLORS

WE MUST NOW SET ourselves to the task of discovering and examining the descriptions of prophetical, political Babylon upon which the indignation of the Lord is to be poured with limitless measure. Nor shall we want for material. The Spirit of God goes to almost unprecedented pains in describing the nation against which He has taken counsel, which counsel He requests us to hear.

A description is a word picture. Like the human artist who applies color after color and executes stroke upon stroke before an image becomes discernible, even so the divine Revealer splashes on the canvas of Scripture words that sparkle with vividness and multiply with frequency. Soon the fundamental image appears with clarity and convincing force. And, as it requires all the colors and all the strokes of the artist to make the picture, even so it necessitates all the descriptives to give us the fundamental image of the nation, spiritually called Babylon, against which the Lord has taken counsel.

There is a striking resemblance between the recorded characteristics of prophetical Babylon and the U. S. A. This will be generally agreed. Some characteristics, however, are more convincing than others. Some are more tenable than others. In the end, they may only strike the reader as an analogy; but, taken as a whole, the consideration is very thought-provoking, and, conceivably, when all the mysteries are unfolded, could prove the U. S. A. to be the very national entity God has in mind.

In such a consideration as this, we are handicapped by prejudice. It is ever distasteful to relate defeat or disaster to oneself, to one's family or to one's nation. Were some foreign national entity in view, say Russia or Cuba, we may not be too strongly predisposed toward sympathy.

Hosea prophesied that "Israel shall bring forth his children to the murderer" (9:13), and "Samaria shall be desolate . . . . they shall fall by the sword; their infants shall be dashed in pieces, and their women with child shall be ripped up" (13:16). At once the populace dubbed him "a fool" and "a mad man" (9:7).

Malachi told the people of his day that God would tear down what they had built in their wickedness (1:4). He told them divine indignation would come upon them (1:4). They quickly reacted in a self-justifying manner: "When have we polluted thee?" they insisted. And there was no change in their conduct. They simply did not believe God meant them.

Ezekiel in his faithful witness for God, said, "Therefore thus saith the Lord God; I will also stretch out mine hand upon Edom, and I will cut off man and beast from it; and I will make it desolate" (Ezekiel 25:13). The people tore at him as thorns and briers. This attitude being so universally true, God asked the question, "To whom shall I speak and give warning?" (Jeremiah 6:10).

We would be well advised to carefully and prayerfully consider in their entirety the descriptions of the nation against which the Lord takes counsel, a nation which is spiritually called Babylon, a nation which will be sorely judged. The brushfuls He applies to the portrayal are vivid and dramatic, and blend into a perceptibly revealing picture.

9. BABYLON'S MOTHER
DESCRIPTION NUMBER ONE

OF ALL THE MULTIPLICITY of descriptives which the Lord gives to make intelligent and convincing the counsel He has taken against a certain Babylon, none seems more logical with which to commence than this: "Your mother shall be sore confounded" (Jeremiah 50:12).

In what sense could historical Babylon have a mother? The city began with a man by the name of Nimrod. In what sense could Babylon the Empire have a mother? It came into the ascendancy of Gentile dominion by divine authority when God interrupted His national dealings with His ancient people. In what sense could Babylon the city have a mother?

Any reputable encyclopedia will reveal that Babylon, the capital of Babylonia, situated on the Euphrates, was one of the largest and most splendid cities of the ancient world, some 1600 years before the Christian era. It was almost entirely destroyed in 683 B.C. A new city was built by Nebuchadnezzar nearly a century later. This city was taken by Cyrus in 538 B.C. and Babylonia became a Persian province at the time of Alexander the Great. The famous city fast declined. The original city was called Shinar by the Hebrews. The contemporary city on the plains of Shinar is Hillah, some 70 miles south of Bagdad. It is clear that the Jeremiah prophecy of Babylon does not have these cities in view when speaking about the "mother of Babylon."

But the Scriptures state that prophetical Babylon has a mother. This "mother-nation" is in existence, though in a deteriorating condition, when prophetical Babylon rises to its apex of glory and incurs the indignation of God. The Bible says she will be "sore confounded." Since this deleterious national condition is concurrent with the full development of the prophesied "daughter," we surely could not imagine the sorely confounded "mother" to be historical Babylon. It is, rather, a kingdom from which this prophesied endtime nation, spiritually called Babylon, has sprung, and is contemporary with it.

Should the U. S. A. be the endtime nation in view in this prophecy, then Britain, by the simplest deduction, would be the mother. And observe, please, Britain is of this hour precisely in the condition mentioned — sore confounded. The word "confounded" means "to pale," "to become dry" (in the vernacular, to dry up, shrink or shrivel), "to lose strength."

On January 16, 1968, the *United Press International* released an article in the news under the caption, "The Nightfall of an Empire." It stated in part, "Britain yesterday abandoned her role as a world power. British Prime Minister Wilson's announcement before the House of Commons came after more than 31 hours of agonizing soul-searching by the British Cabinet."

No longer can the Britisher proudly sing, "Britannia rules the waves," or say with patriotic fervor, "The sun never sets on her possessions." Britain is pale. She is shrinking. Her problems are almost insuperable, her future not too bright.

10. CUP OF GOLD
DESCRIPTION NUMBER TWO

"BABYLON HATH BEEN a golden cup in the Lord's hand . . ." (Jeremiah 51:7). The implications in this verse are many. The "golden cup" is in no sense a chalice (as is true with the "woman" or false church in Revelation 17:4). It is, rather, the thought of a cup of gold, negotiable worth, a means of exchange. We will see later that this prophesied nation, spiritually called Babylon, is a country that has been exceptionally blessed of God.

The idea concerning the "cup" is not only that of a container, but that from which the contents can be poured. The occurrences of the word in the Scriptures are very numerous. Here are some examples:

The cup of salvation — Psalm 116:13
The cup of fury — Isaiah 51:17
The cup of trembling — Isaiah 51:22
The cup of consolation — Jeremiah 16:7
The cup of astonishment — Ezekiel 23:33
The cup of sorrow — Matthew 20:22
The cup of remembrance — Matthew 26:27
The cup of blessing — I Corinthians 10:16
The cup of demons — I Corinthians 10:21
The cup of the Lord — I Corinthians 11:27
The cup of indignation — Revelation 14:10
The cup of fierceness — Revelation 16:19

These references cover a wide area and touch upon various and diversified matters, but the cup of gold in the hand of the Lord commands our attention. The vessel in this instance is not wood, stone or metal substance shaped by some skillful artificer into a utilitarian or ornamental arrangement. It is, rather, a great, God-blessed nation of unprecedented wealth in the whole history of mankind.

And observe carefully where this "cup of gold" once was. It was in the hand of the Lord, that is to say, for His use. And what precisely does God do with gold? We know He utilizes it to pave streets of the glorious city which one day will come down out of heaven and hover above the earth in space, and which will be the home of the bride of Christ (Revelation 21). But what does God do with gold today, in this earthly sphere?

For that matter, what precisely is God doing today in the human realm? He is not now running governments, promoting industry, regulating commerce or controlling finance. This is man's day. God is doing but one thing today. He is calling out a people for His name (Acts 15:14). And God needs gold to accomplish this. True, He owns all the gold as well as the cattle on a thousand hills, but He entrusts negotiable worth with man. Godly men give of their gold to God that His Gospel may be preached to the ends of the earth.

No other nation has rivaled the U. S. A. in sending money and Bibles and missionaries to the ends of the earth. She has indeed been a monetary instrument of Deity in mission endeavor, but a rather alarming connotation attaches itself to the past tense of the verb — "hath been." The implication is that of a changed condition, which condition is of an adverse nature. When godliness decreases, giving to God diminishes. When spiritual devotion wanes, spiritual determination lessens. Today, the fields (of spiritual challenge) which are white unto harvest find the workers pitifully scarce. Mission boards are crying for funds to send the comparatively few candidates they have to the field.

The latest missionary statistics which came to our attention showed that the largest denomination in our land was averaging one lone missionary for twenty churches, while the second largest denomination registered a pitiful six cents per capita per week for missions. Thus, whatever may be the basic thought involved in the verse at hand, it nevertheless presents an apt illustration of an erstwhile generous-hearted nation, now with a lessening financial interest in the work of God.

Where in either sacred or profane history is there any notice of Babylon the empire or Babylon the city pouring money into missionary endeavor? Babylon hindered rather than helped the people of God. It was Babylon which overran the Holy Land and raped it of its treasures. It was Babylon that sadistically gouged out the eyes of Zedekiah, the last king of Judah, but not until they had killed his sons in cold blood before him (Jeremiah 52:9, 10). It was Babylon that caused the Jewish refugees to sit along its rivers and weep (Psalm 127:1). This was, rather, death in the pot" (II Kings 4:40) for God's people and not "gold in the cup" for His cause. There must be some other Babylon in view, or some other nation or kingdom that is spiritually called Babylon which fulfills the implications of the statement made.

11. COSMOPOLITAN COUNTRY
DESCRIPTION NUMBER THREE

"A SWORD SHALL BE UPON . . . the mingled people that are in the midst of her" (Jeremiah 50:37), saith the Lord as He continues to reveal to us the counsel that He has taken against a certain prophetical entity.

The nation God has in view consists of a "mingled people," and is, therefore, cosmopolitan in character. Here we must face the fact that, while this is a striking characteristic of the U. S. A., it could be applicable to other nations as well. However, just because a color has been used in another painting does not mean that it does not find appropriateness in the one being developed. This "mingled people" contribution to the description is a very important one.

The word "mingled" in the Hebrew simply means "mixture" or "mongrel." "Mongrel" is defined as conveying the thought of mixed parentage, mixed origins, or formed of elements from different languages. This is certainly true of the U. S. A. Are we not one from many? Do we not have on our coins "E pluribus unum"? We have all come from some other country, directly or indirectly. Our country is often called the "melting pot."

The word "mingled" carries not only the thought of variety and diversity but strongly connotes integration or assimilation of these varying components into a cooperating and functioning whole. And the one, almost singular factor which makes this descriptive more applicable to the U.S.A. than to any other country is the unilingual aspect. Other countries that are said to be a "mingled people" usually reflect it in a multi-lingual manner. Even our close neighbor, Canada, has two official languages. There is but one official language in the United States, and aliens seeking citizenship are required to speak it. The legal requirement reads, "Applicant must demonstrate an understanding of the English."

More and more our attention is being directed in the area of civil rights. We are reminded that all citizens in this mingled population should enjoy the privileges and opportunities of the land regardless of color, race, creed or national origin. Indeed, minority groups are currently pressing for a fuller enjoyment of these rights which our founding fathers decreed that they should have as citizens.

At any rate, the nation which God is describing is one particular nation. It is one that is cosmopolitan; and, while the term "mingled people" could apply, though with lesser force, to other nations, it must be allowed to register its full contribution to the picture God is painting. In the end, the consummate will furnish the proper perspective.

12. THE YOUNGEST NATION
DESCRIPTION NUMBER FOUR

". . . BEHOLD THE HINDERMOST of the nations shall be a wilderness, a dry land, and a desert" (Jeremiah 50:12).

Without doubt, this is the most poignant reference we have met thus far. It is a striking clue, for "hindermost" denotes the latest or most recent of the nations, the youngest of them all. Most nations were hoary with age when our country was born. In 1968, it was only 476 years since the new world was discovered and a bare 192 years since the U. S. A. was constituted a sovereign state.

We have made fantastic strides in the development of our economy, and momentous advancements scientifically. We have lived so fast and so lavishly that history books are more like fairy tales than cold, unbudgeable facts. It seems but a brief moment from the creeping stagecoach to the supersonic jet; but an insignificant span from the Plymouth Rock hardships to contemporary comforts; but a fleeting shift of the shadow on the sundial from the slate and chalk to electronic computing techniques. The gristmill of vision, patriotism, determination and untiring effort, plus the blessing of Almighty God, has ground out a huge amount of cherished history in an almost minute segment of time. We have risen to an enviable eminence among the countries of the earth.

This phenomenal development is not without explanation, and the explanation sparkles with the vision, courage and dauntlessness of those who, through blood and tears and prayers, fashioned, under God, the greatest and most glorious nation of all time out of a mingled people. They blended cultures and colors of varying and diverse kinds into a common commodity which we proudly call Americanism. We work and worship together. We play side by side; don the same uniform; carry the same flag. Dissident elements, to be sure, like ravishing disease germs in the human system, have plagued the body politic, but the "mingled people" have correlated and synchronized their loyalty, industry and means to make their country and its economy excel all others on the face of the earth.

But, this ethnic infant of which God speaks, like a spoiled child which has been lavished with gifts, is going to be spanked. The Word of the Lord has declared it! "It shall be a wilderness, a dry land and a desert" (Jeremiah 50:12). Even though it is couched in figurative expression, every thinking individual, who hears this counsel as God requested, would understand that this declaration is weighted with a terrifying outcome.

To what Babylon of history could this description possibly apply? The Babylonian Empire was subdued by the Medes and Persians but it did not become a desert. The "hindermost" qualification would obviate conclusively the idea of antiquity.

13. A NATION OF WEALTH
DESCRIPTION NUMBER FIVE

ANOTHER BRUSHFUL GOES on the canvas. The colors are multiplying. The prophet now applies this: "O thou that dwellest upon many waters, abundant in treasures, thine end is come, and the measure of thy covetousness" (Jeremiah 51:13).

Here we have two words, "abundant" and "treasures," pregnant with meaning, each of which suggests rich connotations. "Abundant" is primarily a Bible word. That is, it is more appropriately oriented in scriptural composition. The definitive illustration is that of putting a vessel under a running faucet. The water rises, reaches the brim, then runs over, or abounds.

The word "treasures" does not refer to valuable commodities but to the storehouse containing them. It is the Hebrew word o-tsawr, meaning a depository, an armory, a granary, etc. It is derived from the word aw-tsar which means to store, to lay up in. It adds up to a fabulous amassing of fortunes, and indicates that the nation about which God is speaking is the wealthiest of all nations. This conclusion becomes, seemingly, irrefutably established with subsequent characteristics to be noted.

In this connection, we are reminded that the U. S. A., comprising only 7% of the world's population, is in possession of more than half of the world's wealth. She has 63% of the world's manufactured goods, 74% of the world's automobiles, 52% of the world's trucks, 56% of the world's telephones, 47% of the world's radios, 46% of the world's electric output, 52% of the world's steel and 53% of the world's petroleum.

Our gross national product and income rose from 284 billion 769 million dollars in 1950 to 743 billion 288 million dollars in 1966. This is an astronomical increase in wealth, and singular in the history of nations.

These are fantastic statistics, but they are fraught with an ever-existing danger. In the divine economy is a rigid rule of responsibility — "For unto whomsoever much is given, of the same shall much be required" (Luke 12:48). If this is spoken primarily of an individual, let it be remembered that individuals make up nations, and God speaks of nations forgetting Him, and the serious consequences resulting from this neglect.

We are indeed a forgetful people! Seldom do we think about the price of our heritage. We are an ungrateful people. By and large, we are unmindful of the Bestower of our blessings. Then, too, we have become despicably self-sufficient. We have deified the intellect and exalted man. Revelling in our accomplishments, we are building our "tower of Babel" into the heavens. We are so ego-centric that we have parted company with the Most High God. We are so foolish as to think we can pick a path through the jungle of reason and come out satisfactorily. But not so. It is a course of inevitable failure.

Once the Hon. W. E. Gladstone viewed such a tendency in this way: "One thing frightens me. I am afraid God is dying out in the minds of men." This is the trend in our land today.

He who reveals this counsel about an endtime nation, spiritually called Babylon, unequivocably declares, "Thine end is come, and (together with) the measure of thy covetousness" (Jeremiah 51:13). Thus, it is a nation no longer worthy of divine blessing, one that has bartered away its privileges, and one that shall cease to exist.

14. PRESTIGIOUSLY GREAT
DESCRIPTION NUMBER SIX

THE PICTURE IS DEVELOPING. Here is a vivid brushful: "How is the hammer of the whole earth cut asunder and broken! How is Babylon become a desolation among the nations!" (Jeremiah

50:23). That is to say, Is it not unimaginable that a nation so wealthy and so powerful could be cut off and become an utter desolation?

Take a look at the word "hammer." The verb form means to formulate, to shape or to create as if by hammer strokes; to force or drive as if by repeated blows; to overpower, to overwhelm, or to overrule by persistent force or influence.

Said W. Somerset Maugham, "I wondered if the poor devil had been hammered on the stock exchange."

Webster says, "to make re-iterated effort."

The word "hammer," while connoting force or power, does not here indicate destructiveness. A hammer is not categorized as a weapon, but rather as a tool. The hammer of diplomacy can register telling blows when wielded by a great political power.

No descriptive word in the almost interminable delineation of characteristics is more highly figurative than this particular one. The word "hammer" has a wide application, so wide in fact that there could be as many applications suggested as the number of people applying them. This is one of the many reasons why care should be cautiously exercised and dogmatism restrained in dealing with such matters.

We must be reminded again and again, however, that it has pleased the divine Revelator to couch prophecy in strange but vivid language. The portrayal of the coming world dictator (Antichrist) may at times seem meaningless, even grotesque, such as seven heads and ten horns, but the symbolism sooner or later unfolds into understandable terms. The true meaning will always be obscured in description until sufficient elements combine to make the image unmistakably evident. God gave His Word to convey Truth, and such truth must become apparent or the divine purpose in giving it would be destroyed.

Getting back to the text, it is ever the insatiable desire of the leaders of great nations to use the hammer of influence in strong, far-reaching strokes. Governor Claude Kirk of Florida, representing American governors on a fact-finding mission to Europe regarding monetary difficulties, said, "I think we have to have $70 per ounce for gold with the right of Americans to own it . . . we are the No. 1 nation — we can create the rules" (*Associated Press,* 5/3/68). It requires a strong nation to wield a hammer like that, or to suggest doing so. Imagine a small country like Syria, Lebanon or Iran speaking in this manner.

As the omniscient God looked down through the corridors of

time, He saw the nation, which He is here describing, as wielding the greatest influence of any country—"the hammer of the whole earth." The U. S. A. has unquestionably held that distinction.

15. AMAZING ATTAINMENTS
DESCRIPTION NUMBER SEVEN

"THOUGH BABYLON SHOULD mount up to heaven . . . yet from me shall spoilers come unto her, saith the Lord" (Jeremiah 51:53). Regardless of prophetical Babylon's attainments, her wealth and prosperity, it will be observed how frequently God reiterates the inevitably disastrous end to be experienced.

Of the many meanings for the word "mount," three stand out prominently as having the most pertinence. They are *exalt, excel,* and *increase.* They would seem to present this thought: With enormous technological advances, with abounding natural resources, the increase of productivity and scientific break-throughs, the nation, spiritually called Babylon, will excel all other countries in attaining an exalted position among the peoples of the earth. Russia may have the jump on the U. S. A. in one or two areas, but in the overall picture, our country far excels all others in accomplishments, in wealth and in comfort.

The expression "mount up to heaven" not only has some hints of divine displeasure but suggests a spiritual classification. Was it not Satan, the prince of this world, the instigator of Babylonism, who said, "I will ascend into heaven, I will exalt [myself]" (Isaiah 14:13)? Was it not Nimrod, Satan's chief "advance man," who led his contemporaries in saying, "Let us build us a city and a tower whose top may reach unto heaven: and let us make us a name" (Genesis 11:4)?

Who ever dreamed a few short years ago that the U. S. A. would be spending untold millions of dollars in an attempt to explore outer space and to land a man on the moon? Occasionally the question is posed, Will we ever get a man to the moon? Well, we have the technological know-how, the facilities, and the people's hard-earned money, and, certainly, the determination. And there is no Scripture, to our knowledge, that would indicate this feat cannot be achieved.

We should be reminded, however, that man was created for the earth and not for outer space. That is why, when man leaves the earth, he must take his atmosphere with him. Here are a few expressive verses in point:

> The heaven, even the heavens, are the Lord's; but the earth hath he given to the children of men (Psalm 115:16).
>
> God hath made of one blood all nations of men for to dwell *on the face of the earth,* and hath determined . . . the bounds of their habitation" (Acts 17:26; italics mine).
>
> . . . though they climb up to heaven, thence will I bring them down (Amos 9:2).

God does not say that man shall not attain super-atmospheric goals, but when he does, he will have jumped the divinely-set bounds, and God will bring him down. Just what this actually means is not clear, but it certainly bespeaks ultimate defeat instead of permanent success. Yet, for all of this, the matter of mounting up to heaven may be an overall characterization—an increasing, excelling, exalting condition which spawns pride, haughtiness and forgetfulness of God. Imagination is not required to drape this description about the national attitude of our land.

16. VOICE OF INFLUENCE
DESCRIPTION NUMBER EIGHT

THE DIVINE ARTIST adds a deep color to the emerging portrait of the nation, spiritually called Babylon, when He says, "Because the Lord hath spoiled Babylon, and destroyed out of her the great voice; when her waves do roar like great waters, a noise of their voice is uttered" (Jeremiah 51:55).

It is a clear admission on the highest authority that the nation in view speaks with a great voice; that her pronouncements elicit wide attention; that her expressed suggestions can tip the balance in the direction of her wishes; that her voice is prestigiously regarded; that, alas! the day will come when that voice will be silenced, and that for ever. As a bullet from an assassin's gun can still in a moment the voice of a great leader, even so the judgment from the hand of the Lord will end the voice of the great nation.

Instantaneous global communication and supersonic transportation, buttressed by wealth and power, have encouraged more and more a voice on the part of the U. S. A., not only in matters directly affecting its own interests, but in problems among others as well. We rush envoys to troubled areas to aid in effecting settlements, and usually take the credit when the solution is reached. And all of this may be perfectly sensible in a world which constantly grows smaller and in an era of interdependence. An illustration in point was the recent controversy between Turkey and Greece over Cyprus. Our "voice" was there.

Said U. S. Rep. Thomas L. Ashley, "America has a moral responsibility to maintain global involvement in the world's affairs" (*Toledo News,* 4/28/68).

If the Bible quotation concerning "the great voice" should point up the U. S. A., let it be said with patriotic pride that her voice has been for the most part one of honor; that her commitments have been fulfilled even to the point of sacrificing her beloved sons on foreign soil. But her voice is meeting as never before with bullish opposition by the Soviet Union and her satellites which are slowly rendering it ineffective in international diplomacy. This was especially demonstrated in the Security Council's debate over the Israeli-Arab war of June, 1967. The whole world heard the rebuffs.

But the final articulation of the nation in view will not be that of a famous political power, that for so long sounded forth gloriously in the earth, swaying kings and kingdoms with the hammering strokes of preponderant influence, but, sadly indeed, the roaring cries of a writhing, perishing people whose might will serve as no deterrent in the hour of doom and desolation. This is the inevitable end of the nation about which God has taken counsel.

17. *EXCELLENT FORTIFICATIONS*
Description Number Nine

Our generation is the first in the history of the country to concern itself so prominently about protection from possible enemy attacks. In recent years, the matter of bomb shelters has approached hysteria. Radio network alerts are tested intermittently, and highways all over the country have ominous signs, reading, "Evacuation route." With our avowed enemies possessing devastating weapons in formidable quantities, the fear of attack is ever present, and our leaders have gone to unprecedented ends to establish what they hope will be impenetrable defense systems. The nation God is describing to us is notable for such an effort, but, evidently, to no avail. Here is a solemn entry:

> Though Babylon should mount up to heaven [in technological know-how and in scientific advancement], and though she *should fortify the height of her strength* [do all in her power for self-protection], yet from me shall spoilers come unto her, saith the Lord (Jeremiah 51:53: italics and parenthetical remarks mine).

The word "fortify" means to make inaccessible by height, or restraint. Ancient Babylon had high walls, strong enough to withstand the bombarding of the battering rams and too high for the enemy to vault. Says the *Times Encyclopedia,* "(Ancient) Babylon was in the form of a square, each side 15 miles long, with walls of such immense height and thickness as to constitute one of the wonders of the world."

The intimations of the above prophecy, however, go far beyond stone walls, for prophetical Babylon will be concerned, not about foot soldiers, but about outer space attacks of hostile forces. Thus, she will "mount up to heaven" to the fullest extent of her ingenuity and to the ultimate of her resources. The Strategic Air Command with its intricate and extensive system, for instance, would be an appropriate illustration, indeed a classic example, should it be true the U. S. A. is the nation in view, spiritually called Babylon.

The Strategic Air Command, headquartered at Offutt Air Force Base, Nebraska, is the long-range bomber and missile force of the U. S. Air Force. Its combat-ready air forces can strike anywhere in the world. SAC includes 2nd, 8th, 15th and 16th air forces. It has about 1300 jet bombers and tanker airplanes. SAC uses several types of missiles, including intercontinental ballistic missiles.

SAC's communications network can mobilize the entire command within seconds after a warning. A bomber force can be on the way to its targets within 15 minutes after a warning. If an enemy attack were to destroy SAC's ground control centers, retaliatory attacks would be directed from an airborne command plane. One of these planes is in the air at all times.

For security reasons, there are not many facts and figures available. SAC is but one phase of many precautionary defense measures being developed by the U. S. A., thus reflecting the terrible threat of destructive war in our scientific age. How insufficient would be the protective measures of recent years. The Hindenburg Line, erected by the Germans in 1916 during World War I, across northeastern France from Lille south through St. Gobain, and thence east to Rethel, later to Vouziers and Metz, was thought to be a strong line of defense.

The Hindenburg line and the Maginot wall today would be as useful as a mosquito netting in containing an enraged lion in the face of the nuclear capability of our foes. Thus, as the text intimates concerning prophetical Babylon, our country "fortifies to the height of her strength."

Perhaps a few additional facts on this subject might prove interesting to the reader. The *Nation's Business* (May 1968) asks, "How strong militarily must the United States be in the years ahead? New Defense Secretary Clifford now gives professional military men more say in policies. He sees Red China, rather than Russia, as our main enemy. He's for expanding the nuclear weapons and missile stockpiles.

"Our armed forces and men available for callup total about 3.4 million. In the European theater, NATO forces are slightly under 960,000 Warsaw Pact troops. We have great mobility now. For example, when the fiscal year 1968 orders are delivered, we'll have 7,500 modern turbine helicopters. We now have considerable airlift capability to deploy troops quickly to any part of the globe.

"The Spartan will intercept enemy missiles at altitudes outside the atmosphere. The Sprint will climb thousands of feet in a few seconds, via a gas-pressured getaway technique, and stop objects several miles from target. A new airborne warning system will take care of enemy bombers. Over-the-horizon radars planned for bomber plane defense will also provide for missiles flung from submarines. A satellite-borne missile warning system is in the making." Thus, we "fortify to the height of our strength."

18. WORLD INVOLVEMENTS
DESCRIPTION NUMBER TEN

THAT THE COUNSEL of the Lord is against Babylon, as is plainly stated, is seen more and more in derogatory and denunciatory statements, such as, "O thou that dwellest upon many waters . . . thine end is come" (Jeremiah 51:13).

The idea conveyed by "dwellest," among many other things, is "to set up," or "to establish oneself." The imagination could run widely afield here were it not for the accompanying word "waters." We must keep in mind that we are dealing with prophecy, and in eschatology as well as in other areas of divine Truth, if not more so, we should compare Scripture with Scripture.

Speaking of prophetical religious Babylon, John explained that an angel came to him and said, "Come hither; I will shew unto thee the judgment of the great whore (the composite of religious organizations) that sitteth upon many waters" (Revelation 17:1). Then follows an elucidating statement: "The waters which thou sawest, where the whore sitteth [in Jeremiah "dwellest"] are peoples, and multitudes, and nations, and tongues" (Revelation 17:15).

The above text, Jeremiah 51:13, does not say "upon *all* waters," but rather on "many waters." The Babylon that God has in view is an endtime nation which has in one way or another established herself in many nations.

In this connection, we are reminded that we have military bases, manufacturing plants, oil refineries, offices, etc., in many parts of the world. And, the literal meaning of waters need not be overlooked in this connection. We have warships, aircraft carriers, and naval installations in all the great bodies of water, to say nothing of submarines which ply their way through the seas and the oceans.

There are indeed many ways in which the U. S. A. has connections with many nations. "At present, the United States is committed to help defend 42 nations on every continent except Africa under the eight post-world war II treaties. And in Africa, the U. S. A. is pledged to ponder what action it should take should

Liberia be the victim of aggression. Saudi Arabia has a presidential pledge that its integrity will be protected" (*Montebello News*, 2/15/68).

Such wide-spread involvements as these may point up the reason why so many nations will react mournfully when this prophesied nation comes to her end as is so clearly predicted. "The kings of the earth who have lived deliciously with her shall wail her, and lament for her, when they shall see the smoke of her burning" (Revelation 18:9).

Apparently the conquering force which deals the death blow will release pictures taken by their planes in the aftermath of their triumph, for we read that the people of the earth "shall see the smoke of her burning."

Whatever the identity of the powerful, wealthy nation that falls, can one envision the TV viewing of this unprecedented catastrophe around the world—great cities ablaze as the national economy is hopelessly destroyed? Should it be the U. S. A., can one imagine such an indescribable holocaust—New York City, Boston, Cleveland, Detroit, Chicago, Minneapolis, Atlanta, Houston, Denver, Los Angeles, San Diego, Portland, Seattle, all ablaze?

We of course would hope that this shall not be the fate of our fair land, but, if we believe the Word of God, we must understand that this is precisely what is going to befall some nation. And that nation will answer to the descriptions the Lord has so thoroughly given in His prophetic declaration.

19. FOREIGN AID
DESCRIPTION NUMBER ELEVEN

HERE IS AN ILLUMINATING entry. "The merchants of the earth are waxed rich through the abundance of her delicacies" (Revelation 18:3).

The word "delicacies," which stands alone in New Testament Truth, permits of almost exorbitant connotations. It is the thought of luxury plus voluptuousness. It is a condition which leads to an insensible kind of generosity, such as an inebriated person, with senses confused, wanting to treat everyone regardless of the number or the cost or his ability to foot the bill.

The above Bible text, of course, like the ten previous ones, concerns a nation, and we do not need to overwork our imagination to find an apt illustration.

In an editorial under the caption, "The Global Giveaway," the *Chicago Tribune,** Nov. 2, 1967, commented, "Rep. Otto E. Passman (D. La.), chairman of the House appropriations subcommittee has been advised that the net total of foreign aid through fiscal year 1967 is 114 billion, 694 million dollars.

"Rep. Passman calculates the total cost of foreign aid since 1956, including interest the government paid on money borrowed to give away, as 152 billion, 533 million dollars."

The editorial continues, "New grants and loans to foreign countries now exceed 6 billion dollars a year, and the net total, after all interest and principal payments, is well over 5 billion. Thus the total cost of foreign aid, including interest on the debt, is more than 10 billion dollars a year.

"Rep. Passman charges that the foreign aid program has been 'fragmentized' to confuse the people. He says the aid flows from 16 different 'spigots,' and that each year Congress is asked in more than a dozen items of proposed legislation to increase the spending or lending authority of the dispensing agencies."

The editorial observes, "If the grant aid of 12 billion 928 million dollars extended by the United States under the Marshall plan from 1949 through 1952, and 8 billion 724 million under the mutual security act from 1953 through 1957 had consisted of interest-bearing loans, the prosperous countries of Europe, as well as Japan, would be repaying us now, with interest, and there would be no balance of payments problem. Instead, these countries are accumulating huge gold and dollar reserves and exporting manufactured products at prices with which the United States cannot compete."

The Lord in the long ago revealed that the merchants of the earth would wax rich through the voluptuous luxury and great generosity of an endtime nation, spiritually called Babylon.

The term, "waxed rich," indicates economic assistance to a marked degree, and "of the earth" speaks of the extensive outreach of such liberality. And it must be noted that there is no condemnation in the text because of the distribution of such wealth, for "the Lord loveth a cheerful giver." Yet it is to be expected that, when characteristics are being cited, one of this exceptional type would naturally be prominent in the list. It is of course a chief identifying quality of the U. S. A.

---

* Used by written permission.

20. *BLATANT COVETOUSNESS*
DESCRIPTION NUMBER TWELVE

THE DIVINE ARTIST mixes two deep colors on His pallette as He saturates the brush for this application to the picture which becomes more and more vivid: "It is the land of graven images, and they are mad upon their idols" (Jeremiah 50:38).

The verb form for the word "graven" means to shape, to evolve, to invent. Thus, the nation in view is a land of great inventions. The power to conceive and present new combinations of facts, or ideas, to devise new methods or instruments, encouraged by monetary means, natural resources and favorable opportunity, has flourished in our young democracy. Ours is impressively a land of great inventions, bringing us to the point of a "push button" existence, loading us with benefits undreamed of heretofore. But, while we can computerize ourselves into amazing achievements, we are stalked with the grim specter of spiritual and moral deterioration.

The expression, "mad upon their idols," points to the nation becoming idolatrous and obsessed with her lusts—a lethal kind of diabolical deception which eventuates in spiritual disinterest, disorientation, disunity, degeneration, decadence—disaster. Idolatry is rendered "covetousness" in Colossians 3:5, and covetousness means "wanting more"—the age-long propensity of man. This is reflected both in capital and in labor. Thus, there are strikes, boycotts and athlete holdouts to force a gratification of such insatiable longings.

This condition is undebatably true in America. We live sumptuously but want more. One basketball player this year will receive a salary of $250,000.00 to do in a small part of the year what once was only playful pastime. A 24-year-old girl will get $165,000.00 this year for a few appearances on TV. Any number of baseball players will draw more than $100,000.00 this year. One 1-hour-a-week-for-nine-months TV programs costs $34,000,-000.00 to produce. Other such programs may exceed this figure. All the while, people are in want in our own land and many are starving in other parts of the world.

"Mad upon their idols" reveals an insane pressing for gratification of lusts, with such obsessions destroying all restraints and producing a moral and spiritual breakdown like unto Sodom and Gomorrah. In *Time Magazine* (Nov. '67), Max Lerner is quoted as saying, "America is now living a Babylon existence."

21. EPICUREAN TRAITS
DESCRIPTION NUMBER THIRTEEN

THE COLOR NEXT applied seems to tint the whole portrait. "How much she hath glorified herself and lived deliciously!" (Revelation 18:7). This brushful makes a striking contribution to the desired perspective. It is a general characteristic, poignantly identifying.

"Hath glorified herself" refers to attitude, not to attainment; to personal conduct, not to profitable contribution. The emphasis, at least in God's sight, is comparable with that of historical Babylon, "Let us make us a name" (Genesis 11:4). Prophetical Babylon will have distinguished herself in science, in industry, in commerce, in finance and in art, but will have become woefully independent of God. This, by the very nature of things, even without intent or design, is tantamount to self-glorification, a self-sufficiency which can only eventuate in disillusionment.

Men may scoff at the suggestion, but, as in Jeremiah's day, it is such a course of fleshly enjoyment, flamboyant indifference toward the infinite God, which leads toward the precipice of disaster. The witness of history cannot be silenced. They would not believe God then (Jeremiah 6:10); we will not believe God now. Jehovah pleaded, "Turn ye, turn ye, for why will ye die?" (Ezekiel 33:11). Further, "Amend your ways and your doings, and I will cause you to dwell in this land" (Jeremiah 7:3). And still further, "Repent, and turn yourselves from your idols; and turn away your faces from all your abominations" (Ezekiel 14:6). The reaction of those ancient people was one of stolid indifference and blatant rebellion.

Take a look at the outcome. See them sitting by the rivers of Babylon, weeping, ejected from their land. See the pitiful 500,000 starving to death in Poland. See the 6,000,000 tortured and killed under Hitler. There is no remorse so bitter, or tears of regret so hot, as the kind which could have been averted by man glorifying God rather than glorifying himself.

The "living deliciously" aspect of this description should be an understandable one—a sensual, intemperate, gluttonous kind of habitual sublimation which subjugates all tenets of holy conduct and all rules of proper physical behavior to the unrestrained propensities of desire. This type of comportment flourishes in the climate of prosperity, more so than ever today. "I spake unto thee in thy prosperity; but thou saidst, I will not hear. This hath been thy manner from thy youth (the early days of Israel), that thou obeyedst not my voice" (Jeremiah 22:21).

An illustration in point, so far as our country is concerned may be noted in the exorbitant tab we pick up each year: Americans spend annually for food $84,000,000,000; for recreation $21,-500,000,000; for illegal gambling $47,000,000,000; for alcoholic beverages $11,000,000,000; for tobacco $8,000,000,000; for pets $3,500,000,000; for dog food $210,000,000.

Said a TV reporter just returned from an eastern assignment, "We spend millions for hand lotions and hair tonic while vast multitudes are hungry in India and many are starving." We live deliciously!

A delegate to the World Congress on Evangelism in Berlin made this public statement upon his return: "The Americans were readily distinguishable from the delegates of other nations in two respects. First, in their better dress. Second, in their desire to eat. At the close of the day, some Columbian brethren inquired, 'Where is the nearest prayer room?" while the Americans invariably asked, 'Where is the nearest restaurant?' "

It is not an uncomely trait for people to be neatly and attractively attired. Nor is it unusual for people to experience an urge to eat. But we have moved an alarming distance from the devotion of holy Job who testified, "I esteem the words of thy [God's] mouth more than my necessary food."

What the scriptural description reveals is that prosperity, pride and God-rejection spawn an intemperance, an incontinence, even a moral ruthlessness, which bode ill for any society. It is an index into the human products of apostate times. These are indeed apostate times, and these are indeed the prevailing conditions. If we may use the vernacular, "America is living it up!"

22. *SPIRITUAL DECADENCE*
DESCRIPTION NUMBER FOURTEEN

PROSPERITY LEADS TO SELF-SUFFICIENCY; self-sufficiency leads to spiritual decadence; spiritual decadence leads to moral corruption. Such spiraling incontinence sooner or later reaches heaven; that is, it mounts so alarmingly that it calls down the indictment of God. And here is the divine complaint about the endtime nation which is called Babylon: "Her sins have reached unto heaven (Revelation 18:5).

In a related commentary, this entry should be noted: ". . . she hath been proud against the Lord, against the holy one of Israel" (Jeremiah 50:29). Even the divine appellation in this reference is condemning. When God speaks of His being the "holy One," He thereby intimates incompatibility, that the people are unholy.

That which is against the Lord is sin. Any unrighteousness is sin, and pride in unholy conduct is the forerunner of all indignities against the Most High. It may be under the guise of "new morality" or "situational ethics," but if it is contrary to the divine standards, God categorically condemns it as sin. Sin is not only "a reproach to any people," it is an offense to the Lord.

In a world-wide broadcast recently, the speaker, quoting from a prominent publication, said, "Morals dipped more in 1967 than in the fifty previous years." He was referring to the U. S. A. It could well be that God was speaking of the same nation.

Sordid statistics may only soil the mind, and daily exhibits are everywhere in evidence, but the following may serve as something of an index into our crumbling foundations of morality:

U. S. crime is said to be growing 5 times faster than our population — juvenile crime 7 times faster. Arrests of persons under 18 have increased 10% each year during the past 5 years. In 10 years illegitimate births have increased 300 per cent, and venereal disease has increased 72% in one year. The sale of obscene materials (mostly to children) is more than a million-dollar-a-year business. Prison population is at an all-time peak.

Our crime bill is 20 billion dollars per year. There are said to be 9½ million confirmed alcoholics and an estimated 10 million problem drinkers. Combine all our churches, synagogues and temples, and they are outnumbered by our taverns by 175,000.

A San Francisco newspaper article, with an accompanying photograph, gave this account: "The topless craze stole from the flattering gloom of North Beach nightclubs into the pitiless noonday glare on Broadway yesterday. The girls who paraded with bare bosoms in front of the Peppermint Tree were more studies in sheer show business brassiness than devilish allurement for the neighborhood fleshpots.

"The excuse for it all was an alleged labor dispute involving the management of the Peppermint Tree and 'professional' topless dancers who say they have been aced out of their jobs by zealous 'amateurs.' The complaint is that 14 professionals earning about $150.00 a week were fired two weeks ago to make way for the amazing number of women who are prepared to dance stripped to the waist—for free."

When a thrice-holy God states that "her sins have reached unto heaven," it is an intimation that His longsuffering is being taxed to the breaking point. And when He adds, "She is proud against the Lord," He is indicating the brazenness and boldness with which such sinning is committed before His all-seeing eyes. It is a critical condition, one that can but lead to inevitable judgment, and this is precisely what is predicted for an endtime nation, spiritually called Babylon.

23. EGOTISTICALLY BLIND
DESCRIPTION NUMBER FIFTEEN

AS THE SKILL of an artist produces the finer details of a subject, even so the omniscient Discerner of hearts can translate into verbal expression what humans entertain in their thoughts. It was said of Jesus that "He knew what was in their minds." God knows what is in man (John 2:25). Here is one of the finer but more important details in depicting prophetical Babylon: "For she hath said in her heart, I sit a queen . . . and shall see no sorrow" (Revelation 18:7).

Unlike Hiroshima, Berlin, London, North Vietnam and other unfortunate places, America has never felt the sting of devastating bombs. We sit "a queen." We are the greatest! We are the most powerful! We are the best! Are not these expressive of the general attitude? "It can't happen here" (which seems to be the prevailing thought) is tantamount to the textual expression, "shall see no sorrow." Well, let us not be too sure. Israel had to learn the hard way. Judah likewise. No nation that forgets God can long prosper.

An apostate atmosphere has an acute tendency to dim spiritual vision. Few will take God's pronouncements at face value, but they are always proved to be true. Paul, in that horrifying Mediterranean storm, when neither sun nor moon nor stars were visible for a fortnight, stood amid the 285 sailors on the floundering ship and declared, "Sirs, I believe God that it shall be even as it was told me" (Acts 27:25).

Our foresight is suffering decline rapidly. We ought to know that a society cannot long exist with home life disintegrating, church influence declining and legislative principles departing. Centralized power, corruption in politics, lawlessness in the streets, deficit spending, loss of ideals, disregard for life—these and many other conditions, are destroying the fabric of our national life. Yet we all hope for the best while we espouse the worst. More and more the U. S. A. is assuming a revolutionary posture.

One recently warned, "Our nation is on the skids, at the base of which descent all other nations, taking the same course, have come to disaster." Yet we accelerate our speed in such a course rather than reverse our trends. We "sit a queen . . . . and shall see no sorrow." And so it goes in modern America where the dauntless devotion of Plymouth Rock has given way to a daring departure from all that is high and holy.

The symptoms of decay have been rapidly developing in our young nation. After the assassination of Senator Robert Kennedy, many were the voices diagnosing our fair land as a "sick nation." The President and others tried hard to play down this disturbing inference, but our country is sick. Sin makes any nation sick. Our symptoms are analogous with Israel's, and the Great Physician made this entry in His Record: ". . . . the whole head is sick, and the whole heart faint. From the sole of the foot even unto the head there is no soundness in it; but wounds, and bruises, and putrifying sores" (Isaiah 1:5, 6).

Dr. John B. Streater, pastor of the First Baptist Church in San Francisco, and formerly a missionary in China, writes, "The first time I came in contact with student demonstrations was when I first went out to China in 1947. I remember at the time the reaction was, 'Whoever heard of such a thing! Students who ought to be spending their time getting an education out on the street protesting against the government!' I remember at the time saying, 'Such a thing would not happen in the United States because young people are too busy getting an education.'

"As you know, 1947, '48, '49, were the closing years of the nationalist government and freedom in China, so these student demonstrations were part of the signs of the end of the government in China! In 1949 the Communists took over. All freedom to demonstrate ceased. Freedom of speech, freedom of the press, freedom to own property, freedom to direct one's own life, all of these things—writ of habeas corpus, trial by jury, all became part of a by-gone life!

"It seems it should not be necessary to do a lot of thinking in order to plainly see that the present demonstrations at many of our universities are part of the Communist master-plan to disrupt and destroy our society. Oh yes, they try very hard to camouflage it behind such things as freedom of speech and freedom of the press, but they all follow the same pattern—they are all tied in to the same program." *

We should recall how Israel, in her jubilant but sinful orgies, was warned by the prophet not to rejoice (Hosea 9:1). Disaster for the nation was imminent, and God's servant was trying to turn the people from silliness to sobriety, from foolishness to faith. He was met with despicable disregard. How utterly impossible it seems to be to de-escalate the increasing momentum of a nation toward inevitable catastrophe. This is America today. Because it hasn't happened, we seem to think it cannot happen.

Someone will complain, "Why look for disaster?" The simple fact is, we do not need to look for disaster. It lurks ominously at the end of the wrong course.

24. DISPOSSESSED
DESCRIPTION NUMBER SIXTEEN

AS WE HEAR THE COUNSEL of the Lord against an endtime nation, spiritually called Babylon, a detail is furnished to the por-

---

* Used by written permission.

trayal which strikes to the very center of the national economy. "A sword is upon her treasures; and they shall be robbed" (Jeremiah 50:37). The sword in the text does not speak of an ancient warrior's weapon in felling a foe. It means "to eat down," or more literally "to devour" (*kat-es-thee-o*). What other country has seen so many of the world community ravenously devouring her wealth? A factual illustration may be found in the debts which nations owe us for World War I (which debts have been ignored for fifty years):

Armenia ....$	40,546,970
Austria	25,141,913
Belgium	488,951,077
Czechoslovakia	189,642,023
Estonia	28,080,360
France	5,077,723,883
Great Britain	7,324,459,301
Greece	12,217,376
Hungary	3,105,536
Italy	1,112,473,909
Latvia	11,575,976
Lithuania	10,319,255
Poland	348,334,464
Rumania	82,906,849
Russia	659,940,665
Yugoslavia	51,425,218
Total to 6/30/67......$	15,466,844,782

(From *The World Almanac*, 1968 Centennial Edition)

When the Lord says, "A sword shall be upon her treasures," since a sword connotes destruction, He undoubtedly is speaking of dispossession of her wealth, and He terms it "robbery." The World War I debts are but one lone item that indicates how the nations of the world are depleting our "treasures." What is owed us for World War II, the Korean War, South Vietnam War, together with staggering amounts of goods sent on credit and not paid for should serve to some extent to reveal the type of subtle robbery which is in progress. If one citizen refuses to pay his taxes, rightly due his country, he would be jailed. Why? Because it is robbery.

An editorial in the Chicago Tribune under date of November 2, 1967, states, "Foreign aid is a major reason why your dollar is losing its purchasing power and the debt-burdened, deficit-ridden

United States is in the throes of a money crisis. Foreign aid, including interest on the money we have borrowed to give away, now costs the American people more than 10 billion dollars a year.

"When this unexampled giveaway madness began in 1945, the dollar was still worth 77.3 cents, compared with its purchasing power in January, 1940, in spite of war-time inflation, but by August, 1967, it had declined to 41.48 cents. Meanwhile the United States had accumulated a net deficit of 33.3 billion dollars in its international balance of payments position by the end of 1966; its gold stock had declined from 24.6 billion dollars at the end of 1949 to 13 billion in August, 1967, and its liquid liabilities to foreigners, payable in gold, had increased to 29.5 billion dollars. Now the United States is facing a federal deficit that may exceed 30 billion dollars in this fiscal year, accelerated inflation, and a money crisis that could induce foreigners to start a run on our remaining gold stock. (This, of course, developed as predicted, precipitating a crisis.)

"Moreover, foreign aid is a major cause of federal deficit financing, which increases inflation and the cost of production and thus adversely affects the competitive trade position of the United States."

In 1967, our expenditures exceeded our receipts by almost exactly 10 billion dollars. Any humble, practical-minded person, though not schooled in the intricacies of high finance, would sense that a serious condition exists. Our alarmingly diminishing gold reserves, our deficit spending, our constant giving of what we do not possess, our expensive undeclared wars, our unresponding debtors, the resulting inflation—all lends itself to the divine description in a very telling manner.

The foregoing sixteen descriptions give an enlightening glimpse of the endtime nation God has in view, and concerning which He requests us to hear His counsel against it. He promises that judgment will come, and that it will be severe.

25. LACK OF EMBELLISHMENTS

THE PICTURE IS NOT COMPLETED. There are more descriptions, but the fundamental image seems to be evident, at least developed to the point of usefulness for the purpose at hand. It may be studied for perspective and expression. It is a word portrait silhouetted on the horizon of eschatology, and has to do with a terrifying probability for a particular nation. It is a picture the colors of which blend into a commanding image, and cannot but arrest the careful attention of thinking people.

Should there arise in the reader's mind a question about the abbreviated quotations of Bible references in the foregoing descriptions, may we offer this brief explanation: It was so done, not unwittingly, but with purpose, (1) to conserve space in this limited volume, and (2) to emphasize the descriptive characteristics which might not have been as apparent and as illuminating in the midst of greater verbosity.

In justification of this procedure, we would call attention to the fact that, in many instances in the Sacred Scriptures, an entire verse may not prove to be a completed statement. In Ephesians 1, for instance, it is necessary to cover twelve verses (3 through 14) to complete one full sentence. Yet, it must be granted that it is not uncommon for messages to be built on one of these verses or a fraction thereof. This is not being "partial in the law" (Malachi 2:9), especially when the purpose is properly and accurately served.

More particularly, however, one verse may present two or more unrelated facts, or facts that are widely separated in application. An illustration in point is found in Isaiah 61:2 where a comma divides the verse by more than 1900 years. It is this: "To proclaim the acceptable year of the Lord, and the day of vengeance of our God." The first part of this verse is history; the second, prophecy. In quoting, Jesus used only the first part as He was initiating His earthly ministry (Luke 4:19).

The imaged entity, spiritually called Babylon, does not require embellishment; just sufficient clarity for an assuring identification. Then, we are able to look in the right direction, and to ponder with greater understanding the subject divinely portrayed. We find ourselves then in a position to hear the counsel God has taken against the nation described, which counsel He requests His people to hear and believe. This is the main purpose of this volume.

All the Gentiles will ultimately face the judgment of God for a termination of their national existence (Daniel 2:34, 35); but, we repeat, two powerful countries are definitely singled out for an earlier demise than the others. Russia most certainly is one;

the other is a nation spiritually called Babylon. It is a nation that must inevitably and accurately fit the foregoing description.

Further enlightening details are available. Their inclusion naturally would lend convincing force to our presentation, but space limitations preclude this. It is our wish that the material furnished will add up to a case that will command attention and retain interest. The solemnity of the overall implications is intended not to depress or frighten, but to alert and arouse.

We urgently need to be apprised of the apparent probability which confronts our beloved nation in its ill-advised course, and we must be speedily awakened out of our dreadful indifference toward the holy standards of righteousness which alone can promise a future.

It is not that the author desires to be a self-styled Paul Revere, but he is simply a conscientious sharer of discovered suggestions in the divine Record and a willing transmitter of the same for a timely challenge to those of an open mind. Thus, this matter is presented, not with the thought of provoking argument, but with the hope of producing concern.

26. INSTRUMENT OF JUDGMENT

GOD USUALLY EMPLOYS human instrumentality when executing judgment upon nations, Russia being a striking exception when He will magnify and sanctify Himself without human assistance (Ezekiel 38:22, 23).

Prophecy is that phase of Bible revelation in which God, who knows the end from the beginning, reveals His plans for the future and how those plans will materialize. In the blueprints of eschatology is this specification: "For lo, I will raise and come against Babylon an assembly [alliance] of great nations from the north country: they shall set themselves in array against her" (Jeremiah 50:9).

The immediate reaction will be this: "Then the heaven and the earth, and all that therein is, shall sing [cry aloud] for Babylon, for the spoilers shall come unto her from the north, saith the Lord" (Jeremiah 51:48).

All directions in prophecy, not otherwise indicated, are predicated upon the position of Palestine. South is south of Palestine; north, north of Palestine, etc. Russia is always "north" in prophetic locations. And Russia becomes more and more a threat. Capable of putting launching platforms in space for nuclear missiles, she may be doing so even now. She has also announced that she has the nuclear potential to penetrate all known defense mechanisms.

"The Soviet Union has developed orbital nuclear missiles with devices enabling them to break through an enemy's missile defenses . . . . An orbital weapon is launched like the various spacecraft. It can be brought down on a pre-selected target. The head portions of these rockets carry devices to break through the enemy's antimissile defenses" (*Commercial Appeal*, Memphis, 11/18/67).

The State Department acknowledged the possible truth of this claim. And Russia vows she will destroy the United States.

U. S. News & World Report, July 15, 1968, carries this bold headline: WHY JOINT CHIEFS OF STAFF WORRY OVER U.S. SURVIVAL. Then, the first statement made by General Earl G. Wheeler is to this effect, "The most dangerous threat to the United States is posed by the growing Soviet strategic nuclear forces."

Senator Stuart Symington (Dem.) Missouri, asked this question of General Wheeler, "Are you not beginning, as Chairman of the Joint Chiefs, to become apprehensive about the survival capacity of the United States if things continue along these present lines?"

General Wheeler replied, "The answer is 'Yes,' Senator. You put your finger on what I believe to be the key point, if these trends continue."

A friend, once walking down a street, came upon two lads who were fighting. The one had wrestled his opponent to the sidewalk and was sitting astride him. Amused because the lad on top was crying for help, our friend asked, "Why are you seeking help? You're on top."

"Yes," replied the lad concernedly, "but I feel him rising."

We are on top financially, militarily, and in many other respects, but there is a growing uneasiness, as reflected in General Wheeler's statement, because Russia is rising. Yet, we must not lose sight of the fact, that God Himself is the Agent in invoking terrible and complete judgment on the nation He has described. Whether or not Russia surpasses the U. S. in nuclear ability is really beside the point. One with God is the majority. If U. S. A. is indeed in view, she is doomed!

Observe, further, God says "nations" (plural), and terms them "great." Would He be including China with Russia? What other great country would be ideologically compatible? Both are avowed enemies of the U. S. A. Both have nuclear power. While these two countries seem to be at loggerheads today, there is little question that they would join forces in an attempt to eliminate Uncle Sam.

27. *ENEMY CHARACTERIZED*

IN JEREMIAH 50:42, we read, "They are cruel, and will not show mercy; their voice shall roar like the sea." That is, like Goliath, they will constantly issue threats. Both Russia and China are currently doing this.

And, as for the cruelty of this enemy, it has never been so well known as today. Before the writer are two sizeable booklets printed in the United States Government printing offices in Washington by the Committee on unAmerican activities (House of Representatives, Eighty-six Congress). They both bear the same title, *The Crimes of Khrushchev*. Not only do these publications purport to prove the inhuman character of such godless leaders, but they clearly reveal the vicious attitude of Russia toward the U. S. A.

Said Nikita S. Khrushchev in Warsaw, April 1955, concerning the United States (and a whole page is given in one of these booklets to this quotation), "We must realize we cannot co-exist for a long time. One of us must go to his grave. We do not want to go to the grave. They [meaning Americans] do not want to go to their grave either. So what can be done? We must push them to their grave."

Following are a few excerpts from these booklets:

"Mr. Arens: Would you sum up briefly your judgment of Khrushchev and his impending visit?

"Mr. Lyon: I'll try. In the first place, the new Soviet boss, despite his homespun exterior, is one of the bloodiest tyrants extant. He has come to power over mountains of corpses. Those of us who roll out the red carpets for him will soon have red faces."

The daughter of Josef Stalin, who defected to our country, has given in writing something of the brutality of her father.

Now take note of this nauseating statement by the leader of the Communistic Party in this very land of ours. "I dream of the hour when the last Congressman is strangeld to death on the guts of the last preacher—and since Christians seem to love to sing about the blood, why not give them a little of it? Slit the throats of their children and drag them over the mourner's bench and the pulpit, and allow them to drown in their own blood; and then see whether they enjoy singing these hymns" (*Sword of the Lord,* 4/20/62).

Says *U. S. News & World Report* (July 15, 1968), "Never in modern history have prisoners of war been treated the way Americans are treated by the Vietnamese Communists. Reds in Vietnam defy the accepted rules of warfare. Prisoners are isolated, often abused, rarely identified by the enemy.

"Torture has been used to try to make prisoners talk. In one form, a man's ankles are bound and his legs pulled up behind him. The other end of the rope is looped around his neck. A man who struggles or tries to straighten his cramped legs runs the risk of strangling himself."

Did God exaggerate when He said this enemy is cruel? Does God ever exaggerate? *Never!*

28. NATURE OF ATTACK

1. *It will be sudden—a sneak attack.* "O Babylon, thou wast not aware; thou art found and also caught" (Jeremiah 50:24). Analyze these words. "Not aware" means complacent, self-assured. "Thou art caught" means the enemy breaks through her defenses. "Caught" spells *finis.* This is her demise, and God has already written her obituary.

2. *Paralyzing sabotage.* "The passages are stopped . . . and the men of war [military leaders] are affrighted" (Jeremiah 51:32). "Passages" probably suggests means of communication, and the word "stopped" means "to cut off." Radio, television, telephone and telegraph can be cut off suddenly—all perhaps accomplished by a national blackout of electricity. This is a painful possibility. We had an alarming taste of such an experience a year or more ago in the New York City area, with confusion, inconvenience and frustration indescribable. Multiply this by continent-wide proportions. What would be the reaction?

The statement says, "Men of war affrighted." This word has strong suggestions, such as, tremble inwardly, be alarmed, to hasten, to be anxious, to be amazed, to be dismayed, to be troubled, to be vexed. If such a situation were to develop in our fair land, not only would national and civic leaders be frustrated, but military personnel would be discomfited. And something of this nature *will*, verily, happen to some great nation.

3. *The enemy's effective strategy.* "Their arrows shall be as a mighty expert man; none shall return in vain" (Jeremiah 50:9). The missiles, like perfectly aimed arrows, will not miss their targets.

4. *Total devastation will ensue.* Note this solemn divine declaration: "Babylon is suddenly fallen and destroyed" (Jeremiah 51: 8). Not just defeated; not just hurt; but destroyed! Sounds utterly inconceivable for any nation, and unthinkable for the U. S. A. But it may be the confronting probability.

5. *An irreparable loss.* To make this a bit more understandable, the Spirit directs our attention to a former day when His hand of judgment fell: "As God overthrew Sodom and Gomorrah and the neighboring cities, saith the Lord" (Jeremiah 50:40). If we can read this aright, the nation in view will be left a shambles, totally uninhabitable, together with adjacent cities (countries), not only because of wanton, unimaginable destruction, but also, apparently, because of radioactive fall-out.

6. *World-wide reaction.* This indescribable catastrophe will be lamented far and wide: "And the cry is heard among the nations" (Jeremiah 50:46). Again in Revelation 18:11, "The merchants of the earth shall weep and mourn over her." The reader would experience much difficulty in trying to convince himself that this has to do with ancient Babylon.

7. *Rapidity of this devastation.* This catastrophic judgment will be over in one hour. "Alas, alas, that great city Babylon; that mighty city [nation], for in one hour is thy judgment come . . . For in one hour so great riches is come to nought . . . For in one hour is she made desolate" (Revelation 18:10, 17, 19). We have no choice but to construe this thrice-repeated "hour" as literal. The swiftness of the Israeli-Arab war (June '67) will seem in comparison like an eon. This is the destructive potential of present-day nuclear weapons.

The *Nation's Business* (May 1968) reveals that "Russia apparently is flight-testing in secret a means for putting warheads into orbit to float menacingly through space until the Soviet Union is ready to drop them. The capability to station bombs indefinitely in space creates a new sophisticated weapon we'd have to contend with.

"Russia already has developed what's called a fractional orbital bombardment system which puts a warhead into a low orbit to be ordered down before it completes a full circuit."

In citing these chilling statistics, we are not intimating that our leaders, charged with the defense of our country, are asleep at the switch, or that they are in any way remiss in attempting to meet these mounting threats. They have done and are doing a great deal more than can be made public. Nor are we willfully pessimistic, but when the infinite God, who stakes His holiness on the integrity of His Word, says a nation will go down under His mighty hand of judgment, there is no defense. And so it will be for a certain endtime nation, spiritually called Babylon—a country that gambles on its own strength and forsakes God.

If the wealthy, powerful, wicked, God-forsaking endtime nation, spiritually called Babylon in prophecy, and which is to be visited by this devastating judgment, is indeed the U. S. A., then perhaps this is the answer to the oft-raised question, "How can Russia, the king of the north" (Daniel 11:40), invade Israel without American protest or intervention? Of course, in such an event, though hideous the thought, she would no longer exist.

29. TIME OF DEVELOPMENT

TIMETABLES IN PROPHECY are not always readily deciphered. We are sometimes forced to view patterns of prophesied developments, and then to correlate the factors within the given pattern. This we know, however, the divine plan, among other important matters, calls for the elimination of Religious Babylon, Political Babylon* and Russia, and, we believe, in this precise order. Thus, if God is going to use Russia to destroy prophetical, political Babylon, then obviously political Babylon must go down before Russia is eliminated. Then, when will Russia be eliminated?

* That prophetical, political Babylon is contemporary with the ultimate development of the false Church and modern Russia is a powerful proof that the Babylon prophesied in Jeremiah 50 and 51 and Revelation 18 is this projected entity.

Since Russia will be supernaturally disposed of at the time of her invasion of Palestine and Egypt (Ezekiel 38:22; Daniel 11: 40-45), and if we are justified in believing that the Antichrist (world dictator) is at that time mortally wounded and resurrected (Revelation 13:3, 12), and since power is given to him (the Beast returned from perdition, Revelation 11:7), to "continue for forty-two months" (Revelation 13:5), or the whole of the second half of Daniel's 70th week, then Russia's demise will be before the first half of the week ends, most likely toward the middle of Daniel's 70th week.

The judgment of the nation, spiritually called Babylon, must precede the downfall of Russia if Russia is to be God's instrument of judgment, and the end of religious Babylon (the ultimate of organized religion) will have taken place earlier. The time, then, for prophesied political Babylon's desolation will be sometime in the first half of Daniel's 70th week.

This leads us to a very logical and a most re-assuring conclusion—the true Church will not be here at that time. She will have been evacuated — raptured (I Thessalonians 4:16, 17)! That is not to say she shall not see hard times. Pressure is constantly being brought to bear upon the people of God, but the Church shall certainly be spared from this inevitable national disaster.

Further, if the U. S. A. is eliminated by Russia, Russia's ultimate defeat must of necessity be supernatural (Ezekiel 38:22, 23), for there would be no earthly power capable of subduing her. Assuming that the U. S. A. is removed from the scene, Communism's only obstacle, then, to world domination would be Antichrist and his rising ten-kingdom power out of Europe. Hence, the "king of the North" (Russia) will push at him (Antichrist) as found in Daniel 11:40. At that time, the King of Glory will step into the picture, will put hooks into his jaws (Ezekiel 38:4), and will destroy him utterly (Daniel 11:45; Ezekiel 38:22, 23).

Antichrist, or the world's worst and last dictator, will prosper in his unprecedented nefarious acts till he is destroyed by the Lord in His second advent (II Thessalonians 2:8).

This is something of the format of divine plans in ridding this earth of its rebellion and sin.

30. A PROMINENT NAME

THE WORD "BABYLON" IS LEGENDARY. When it appears in print, or falls from a speaker's lips, myriads of concepts flash across the screen of one's thoughts. There is the Tower of Belus with the fantastic dreams of its erectors—a tower pushing heavenward. Or,

There is the ancient empire with Nebuchadnezzar enthroned in his glorious dominion as the head of gold, the initial monarch, holding a scepter over the whole world in Gentile sovereignty. Or,

The great city which etched itself into the fabric of history with an almost singular design, the center of commerce—the envy of mankind. Or yet,

A woman arrayed in purple and scarlet, decked with gold and silver and pearls and scintillating gems, holding a golden chalice— the fantasy of ecumenicists, a dream come true for religionists. Or even yet,

An ethnic entity with blazing colors of grandeur, fabulous in her wealth, unrivaled in her scientific achievements, obsessed with her lusts, transcendent in her power.

But all that has the *hallmark* of Babylon must be purged from the earth. And God will do it! As for historical Babylon, He said, "Go to, let us go down, and there confound their language . . . So the Lord scattered them abroad" (Genesis 11:7, 8).

As for religious Babylon (the final form of religious organization), the ten-horned kingdom of Antichrist will outlaw it, and destroy it, and expropriate its vast resources (Revelation 17:16), "for God hath put it in their hearts to fulfill His will" (Revelation 17:17).

And, as for political Babylon, a powerful, prosperous, prestigious endtime nation, she will go down to destruction even as went the "woman" (Revelation 17:18), and the agent in this regard, as in all other instances, is none other than God Himself. "From me shall spoilers come unto her, saith the Lord" (Jeremiah 51:53).

That the stamp of Babylon and the subtlety of Babylon and the stigma of Babylon must be completely eradicated should be most evident to those who know the Scriptures. As was pointed out earlier in this volume, the basic concept in the Babylon doctrine is twofold. First, to contradict all that God says; and, second, to counteract all that God does. Nor does it matter whether this satanic subtlety is inherent in a religious body or in a nation. It is anti-Christ, and "He [Christ] must reign till *all* enemies are put under his feet" (I Corinthians 15:25).

As the word "Baal" became colloquial in Old Testament times as referring to all types of idolatry (usually in the plural, Baalim), even so the word "Babylon" throughout the ages has been employed to connote intemperance, lustfulness and unspirituality. Journalists speak of America as "living a Babylon existence."

The total triumph of our blessed Lord guarantees the elimination of everything which militates against His holiness. He will purge the holy of holies of the foul presence of the image of the Antichrist. He will cast the devil into the lake of fire. He will purge out the rebels of Israel (Ezekiel 20:38). He will judge the Gentile nations, turning the unbelieving into everlasting destruction. He will remove the curse from the earth.

All of this purging and purifying in His redemptive scheme would not and could not be complete if the whole Babylon issue were not settled fully and for ever.

This will not be accomplished in one stroke of judgment. The divine plan, clearly set forth, calls for, among other things, the termination of religious Babylon, the final form of church organization with all its confusing and empty doctrines, and the destruction of political Babylon which is a God-blessed endtime nation that gradually but surely ruled the Lord of glory out of its national structure.

31. A RECAPITULATION

THE PERIOD OF GENTILE DOMINION had a specific beginning (Daniel 2:37). This period will have a definite termination (Daniel 2:34). It is firmly established and plainly revealed that the Lord of glory will wind up the affairs of the nations, and will Himself institute His own government and reign in righteousness over the whole earth (Isaiah 2:4). It is noteworthy in this connection, however, that the Spirit of Truth lists certain nations to fall by divine judgment prior to the total collapse of Gentile dominion which will take place when our Lord returns to this earth.

Particularly cited, are two great sovereign states which will have especially incurred the indignation of the Lord. The one is "the king of the north" or Russia (Ezekiel 38:22). But prior to this nation's demise, another of even greater prominence is slated for the consuming vengeance of the Lord. This nation is spiritually called "Babylon."

Historical Babylon is to eventuate in two imposing branches, viz., religious Babylon, the ultimate of organized religion, and prophetical, political Babylon, a powerful but God-forsaking endtime nation.

God will put it into the hearts of Antichrist's ten kingdoms to utterly eliminate the "woman" or the false church, which is religious Babylon (Revelation 17:16, 17). He also will take counsel against prophetical, political Babylon and will cause great nations from the "north" to destroy her.

Before this judgment falls, God will call for His people (those saved in the early part of Daniel's 70th week) to flee this doomed nation and emigrate to Zion or Palestine (Jeremiah 50:28).

Since unnamed entities in prophecy may be identified by description, and since this endtime nation is not specifically named, we are obliged to search for its description which, obviously, is quite prolific. Some of the given characteristics are as follows:

1. She is the offspring of a kingdom which will deteriorate from a position of world leadership.

2. She at one time was a cup of gold in the Lord's hand—a monetary instrument in the promotion of God's work.

3. She has a cosmopolitan population—a "mingled people."

4. She is the latest or youngest of nations, said to be "the hindermost."

5. She is an exceedingly wealthy country—"abundant in treasures."

6. She is the most powerful nation and termed "the hammer of the whole earth."

7. Her scientific achievements excel all other nations.

8. She speaks with an influential voice in the world community.

9. She has established unprecedented national defenses.

10. She involves herself in global affairs.

11. She is singularly and lavishly generous in foreign aid.

12. She has the highest standard of living, even of an epicurean character.

13. She becomes a spiritual renegade, lapsing into idolatry and covetousness.

14. Through unrestrained permissiveness, a moral decadence ensues to the proportions of blatant turpitude.

15. She develops pride and haughtiness through egotistical bias and claims to "sit a queen," untouched by defeat and untouchable.

16. The "unsinkable titanic" of nations is slowly, subtly and surely stripped of her gold.

Some endtime nation will answer to these descriptions. That nation, having been mightily blessed of God, will incur His indignation because of her godlessness. And when the hour of divine judgment arrives, an alliance of great nations from the prophetical "north," possessing devastating, vulnerable weapons in formidable quantities, will strike unexpectedly, suddenly and decisively.

As the "woman" (the false church) shall be utterly eliminated, even so, the endtime nation, spiritually called Babylon, shall irreparably perish from the earth. Her beauty and pride shall no more restrain the hand of divine judgment than the impressiveness of Lucifer, the son of the morning, could prevent his fall and ultimate doom when he turned from God and, through pride, exalted himself.

32. NOT AN EMPTY THEORY

IT WOULD SEEM most improbable for one, no matter his hermeneutical knowledge or exegetical ability, to compress all the Babylon matter of Jeremiah 50 and 51 into the mold of history and label it "Fulfilled."

Thus, this image of an endtime nation, spiritually called Babylon, is more than a mirage on the surface of an author's imagination. It is there irrefutably and irremoveably on the pages of Sacred Writ. The Holy Spirit has painted the picture. Its colors are true. Its brushstrokes are accurate. The fundamental image is established for all who have eyes to see. The perspective is clear.

However, since similarities at times may be coincidental rather than substantiating, we may be reluctant to title the portrait in terms of a modern nation. But no one can lightly dismiss completely the possibility of its being the nation which we love. We do not avow that it is. On the other hand, with the facts thoroughly pondered, one would hesitate to declare flatly that it is not.

On what comfortable and convenient grounds can the U. S. A. claim immunity from divine judgment? "The nation that forgets God goes backward"—backward to defeat, backward to destruction. That we as a nation are going backward cannot be denied. We are regressing spiritually, morally, legally, financially, governmentally, and that with alarming acceleration. It is only natural, of course, to abhor any suggestion of national disaster. This was the bitter reaction of the people in Jeremiah's day. He prophesied with great compassion that judgment would befall the nation, that the "city of peace" would be razed. He was cast into a miry dungeon by angry mobs who were vociferous in denying that such a thing could be true and in claiming that the preacher was suffering from a neurosis. But it *did* come to pass!

The Lord told Daniel in stranger language than he employs in Jeremiah 50 and 51 and in Revelation 18 that judgment would come to his nation. The picture was painted in complicated imagery. There was a little horn, a ram, a goat, etc. There was also the king of fierce countenance, the terrible Antiochus Epiphanes. In spite of the striking visions and stirring imagery, Daniel knew that God was telling him something actual, something severe; that catastrophic judgments would come. He believed God. He knew that horrendous developments were in the offing, and this was his reaction: "I Daniel fainted, and was sick certain days . . . I Daniel was grieved in my spirit . . . my countenance changed in me."

One is not a prophet of gloom, a pestilential pessimist, a draper of dismay, or a crepe hanger who believe's God's judicial pronouncements and dares to make them known. General aversion to such facts furnishes no escape, nor is violent objection in any wise a detente. God's justice cannot be deterred. "He is faithful who hath promised and he will do it."

Said the renowned Gen. William K. Harrison, "I do not know a nation of modern times that deserves the judgment of a holy God as much as America. No other nation has been granted such physical blessings, such spiritual opportunities and such political freedom, yet it has become pagan in character." Divine judgment of some form seems inevitable.

33. A GLIMPSE OF MODERN AMERICA

THE PORTENTS ON THE HORIZON are most disturbing. The fierce clashes of conflicting ideologies, ruthless subversive tactics, the violent quest for power, the uprisings of minorities—all combine with myriads of other disconcerting factors to becloud the atmosphere.

Add to this the current racial demonstrations, the restlessness of the underprivileged, together with the constant increase of immorality and crime, of corruption in high places, of multiplying espionage agents which can be counted but not captured, the prevailing lawlessness, the looting of property, the burning of cities, the disintegration of home life, the prevalence of juvenile delinquency, the fickleness of fads, the rapidly declining influence of the Church. The picture is a somber one!

And the outlook is not bright. An article in the *St. Petersburg Times* of December 14, 1967, stated in part, "In order to assure itself of large audiences, television must rely on adult pictures with their increasing emphasis on sex, nudity, and violence. In short, when the issue comes down to a choice between profit and morality, profit in the long run almost always wins. It is just a question of time before anything goes."

The more alarming way to put it is this: It is only a question of time before such a nation, as did Sodom and Gomorrah, goes down under the hand of divine judgment, and for the same reason.

Lord Byron said, "Civilization goes like this: First freedom, and then glory, and then wealth, and then vice, and then corruption, and then barbarism, and then collapse."

Whatever he may have had in mind, the late President Kennedy said in his state of the Union message, "Each day we draw nearer to the hour of maximum danger."

Dr. Robert Munger put it this way: "We stand at the crossroads of destiny confronted by a chaotic world on the brink of self-destruction."

Dr. Robert Schuler adds, "The survival of America is at stake."

There is a growing universal obsession that finite man with

advanced technological knowledge, supersonic transportation and instantaneous global communication can bring about a *Utopia* on this earth. It is a grandiose scheme—appealing, challenging, convincing. It calls for *one* world, *one* government, *one* church, but this enlarging bubble is doomed to burst.

The Bible states that when they shall say, "Peace and safety, then sudden destruction cometh upon them as birthpains upon a woman with child." Man has neither the foundation on which to build such a glorious situation nor the right kind of material. "A society predicated on a false premise is pre-doomed" (Paul Harvey). And history is replete with examples—civilizations buried under their own ruins.

Make no mistake, the great and pressing need of the hour for us as individuals and as a nation is to get back to God—back to the deep, rich things of His holy provision, back where the soul of man can find rest in the rush of our frustrated age, back where the heart can find confidence as foundations crumble about us. And the way back to God is the way of His Book. It is, and ever shall be, "a lamp unto our feet and a light unto our path." Its hallowed illumination leads into the way "of the just which shines more and more unto the perfect day."

It may be the eleventh hour, but many a fight has been won in the last round. If the reader does not know God's plan for his personal salvation and his spiritual responsibility to others, ascertain it speedily! Then, with vigor, courage and honesty, as should all true believers, fight the good fight of faith. Victory is not only preferable to defeat, it is absolutely possible under God!

If our nation would turn to God and honor His Word, there would be no question about her future. *But* if the present trends continue and increase, she may possibly be the endtime nation to be judged.

It is not our purpose in this presentation to render a verdict or to finalize a conclusion, but simply to adduce evidence. Evidence is the material of proof. Whether or not the proof is irrefutably established in this case, the reader/hearer must determine for himself. However, one disturbing question will linger on the horizon of our minds—to what other nation of all time could these divinely-given characteristics and descriptions so convincingly apply?

Those of us whose heartbeat is quickened by the singing of "America the Beautiful" could wish that the endtime nation to be destroyed is not the U. S. A. Those of us whose spirits are moved to see Old Glory waving in the breeze as the martial strains of the National Anthem fill the air are wont to cry, "Perish the throught!" But who amongst us is not painfully aware that our great Ship of State is currently in turbulent waters and headed for treacherous shoals? Concern prevails!

View matters as one will, the only security for the individual is in the Saviour and His salvation. The unbeliever should take refuge through faith while there is time, place and opportunity. Those who do believe should evidence stronger faith and devotion, and, "having done all, to *stand!*"